J. J. McCarthy

A Child's Story of the Bible

J. J. McCarthy

A Child's Story of the Bible

ISBN/EAN: 9783337171902

Printed in Europe, USA, Canada, Australia, Japan

Cover: Foto ©Lupo / pixelio.de

More available books at **www.hansebooks.com**

A CHILD'S
STORY OF THE BIBLE

ENTERING THE ARK.

ALTEMUS' YOUNG PEOPLE'S LIBRARY

A Child's

Story of the Bible

WITH 72 ILLUSTRATIONS

PHILADELPHIA
HENRY ALTEMUS
1895

> IN UNIFORM BINDING
> PROFUSELY ILLUSTRATED
>
> ROBINSON CRUSOE
> BUNYAN'S PILGRIM'S PROGRESS
> A CHILD'S STORY OF THE BIBLE
> A CHILD'S LIFE OF CHRIST
> ALICE'S ADVENTURES IN WONDERLAND
> THROUGH THE LOOKING-GLASS

Copyrighted, 1895, by HENRY ALTEMUS

HENRY ALTEMUS, MANUFACTURER
PHILADELPHIA

INTRODUCTION

THE present volume endeavors to tell in simple language, and in a form fitted for the hands of the younger members of the Christian flock, the tale of God's dealings with his Chosen People under the Old Dispensation, with its foreshadowings of the coming of that Messiah who was to make all mankind one fold under one Shepherd. The words are simple, so that all can understand them without difficulty. Our efforts have been directed to make this book not only attractive to the little ones, but of assistance to those who have the privilege of introducing them to the inspired accounts of the world's history from its Creation to the sorrowful death and glorious ascension of our divine Saviour Jesus Christ.

The title of the BIBLE is derived from a Latin word, itself derived from the Greek, which signifies "Book," and was applied to the Hebrew Scriptures as well as to the New Testament, as being books read in Christian Churches. It comprises the Five Books of Moses, or the Law, the Historical Books, the Prophetical Works, and Devotional Works. By the Law is understood Genesis, Exodus, Leviticus, Numbers and Deuteronomy. The Historical Books comprise the Books of Joshua, Judges, Ruth,

Samuel, Kings, Chronicles, Ezra, Nehemiah and Esther. The Prophetical Works are the prophecies of Job, Isaiah, Jeremiah, Ezekiel, Daniel and the Twelve Minor Prophets; while under the head of Devotional Works are the Psalms, Proverbs, the Song of Solomon and Ecclesiastes.

The Old Testament is but the Introduction to the New Testament. The creation of the world, as told in the Book of Genesis, the Bondage in Egypt, the Conquest of the Promised Land, the picturesque and dramatic history of the Chosen People, of their Judges and Kings, their Warriors and Statesmen, their Priests and Prophets, their Captivity in Babylon, and their Return to their native land, all point forward to the Story of the Redeemer, all serve but to prepare the way for the Coming of Christ, the Saviour of the World. The books which we know as constituting the OLD TESTAMENT are, also, counterparts to those that constitute the NEW TESTAMENT. The Four Gospels correspond to the Pentateuch or the Five Books of Moses, the Acts of the Apostles to the Historical Books, the Epistles to the Prophetical Works, and the Book of Revelation to Daniel and Ezekiel. The Old Testament is the Covenant of God with his Chosen People, the New Testament speaks of the New Covenant of God with all Mankind, by which all are offered the privileges of adoption as Children of God and Heirs of the Kingdom of Heaven.

With the exception of Daniel, which is written in Chaldee, the Canonical Works of the Old Testament are in the Hebrew language, spoken by the Jews in the Holy Land. But in addition to these Canonical

Scriptures, there are several historical narratives written in Greek, which the greater part of the Christian World hold in high esteem, and which are read for "instruction in manners." These Apocryphal Works, as Protestant Churches call them, were written after the Jews had been led away captive into Babylon and form the connecting link between the Old and New Testaments. They are of great historical value, as telling us of the struggles of the Jews under the Greek Kings of Syria.

Of all these works various translations in many languages have been made. The Hebrew text was rendered into Greek about 300 years before the birth of Christ, and all were translated into Latin about the second and third centuries of the Christian era. The revision of this Latin Version by S. Jerome (A. D. 383) became the Authorized Version of the Western Church, and is called the *Vulgate*. From this Latin Version partial translations were made into the vernacular languages of various countries, and a version of the whole into English appeared under the name of Wyclif about 1382. After the introduction of printing into England, in 1477, other translations, summaries and extracts were given to the world, and in 1535 the first complete English Bible was issued by Miles Coverdale. In 1611 the so called "authorized" English version was published, and this was carefully revised by companies of English and American scholars during the years 1870 to 1880, the result being known as the "Revised Version." The New Testament, thus revised, was published in 1880, the Old Testament in 1884.

ADAM AND EVE DRIVEN OUT OF THE GARDEN OF EDEN

THE STORY
Of the Old Testament

CHAPTER I

THE CREATION—THE FIRST MAN AND WOMAN—
ABEL KILLED BY CAIN—THE DELUGE—THE
CALLING OF ABRAHAM—THE BIRTH OF ISAAC.

IN the beginning God made all things, and on the sixth day he looked upon what he had made; and he was well pleased with it. And he rested on the seventh day, and made it holy.

God formed man from the dust of the ground, in his own image, and breathed into his nostrils the breath of life. And God spoke kindly to Adam ("The Man"), and told him that he should have power over every living thing on the earth, the birds in the air, and the fish in the sea. The fruit on the trees and bushes was to be his food, and he was placed within the beautiful garden of Eden, to dress it and to keep it. A river passed through the garden to water it. And Adam was to eat of every tree in it, except the Tree of the Knowledge of Good and Evil. If he ate of this tree, he would surely die. And God saw it was not good for man to be alone, so he made Eve out of a bone from Adam's side, and gave her to him to be a wife or helpmeet. And all the animals which God had created came to Adam, and he gave them their names.

Although everything was so beautiful, and although Adam and Eve were good, and perfectly happy, the Devil came in the form of a serpent, and told Eve that there would be no harm in tasting the fruit upon the forbidden tree. And she looked at it, and believed the serpent; and stretching forth her hand, she plucked the fruit and ate it, and also gave to her husband. As soon as they had eaten of the forbidden fruit they knew they were naked, and went and hid themselves. Then God asked them why they had done this; and they were both afraid. And Adam laid the blame upon his wife, and she blamed the serpent. But God was displeased with them both, and he cast them out of the beautiful garden, and cursed the ground for their sake; and he told them they would have to work hard for their bread, and after this their bodies were to die, and return to the dust. But God promised that he would afterwards send a Saviour, who would save them and their descendants from the guilt of their sin, if they would believe upon him.

And God gave Adam and Eve two sons after they were driven out of the garden. The name of the

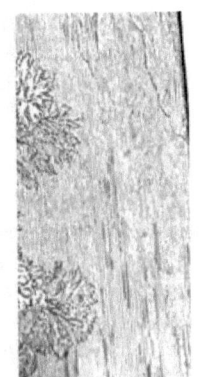

elder was Cain, and of the younger Abel. Cain worked as a farmer or gardener; but Abel was a shepherd. And one day they offered up a sacrifice to God: Cain's offering was the fruits of the ground, that of Abel was a little lamb. Now Abel was sorry for his sins, and God heard and pardoned him. But Cain continued hard and stubborn. And Abel's sacrifice was accepted by God, but that of Cain was not. This made Cain very angry. And God asked him why he was angry; if he did right he would be pleased with him, if he did not do right it was his own fault.

This made Cain envious of Abel, and one day he rose up against him in the field and slew him. And God called him, and asked where his brother was. Cain said he did not know; was he his brother's keeper? And because Cain had done this God set a mark upon him so that every one would know him, and sentenced him to be a fugitive and a wanderer for the rest of his days. Then Cain built a city in the land of Nod, to the east of Eden, and amongst his descendants were Jabal, Jubal, and Tubal-cain. Jabal taught people to dwell in tents and keep cattle; Jubal taught the art of music; and Tubal-cain was skilful in making articles out of brass and iron.

Enoch, a descendant of Seth, another son of Adam, was a very good man, who passed from earth to heaven without dying. He walked with God; and he was not, for God took him. His son Methuselah lived longer than any man either before or since; he was nine hundred and sixty-nine years old when he died. Many years afterwards the people began to increase upon the earth. And they were very wicked, and did what pleased themselves, and never thought about pleasing God; so he determined to punish them. He said his Spirit would not always strive with man, but that after a hundred and twenty years man would be destroyed.

And God spoke to a good man called Noah, the grandson of Methuselah, and commanded him to build an ark, a large house that might float upon the waters. And Noah did so; but it took him about one hundred years to build it, and all the people that passed by mocked him, and said what a fool he was to take so much trouble in building such a large floating house. But Noah knew better, and believed God. And one day God told him to come inside the ark with all his family, and to take some of all kinds of birds and beasts with him. And Noah and his family and all the animals entered the ark, and God shut them in. As soon as Noah and his family were inside the ark it began to rain, and it rained for forty days and forty nights. And everything outside the ark was covered with water, so that even those who went to the tops of the highest hills were drowned. Everybody and every living thing that was left outside the ark perished in that great flood.

After forty days Noah opened a window in the ark and let a raven fly out, in order to see if there was any dry ground; but the raven returned, having found no place to rest upon. Then he sent forth a dove, but she also returned; then he sent forth the dove again, and she went away for a whole day, but in the evening she returned with an olive leaf in her mouth. Then Noah knew that the waters were abating. The next time the dove was sent out she did not return. God did not forget Noah, and after his time was accomplished the ark rested on Mount Ararat. Everything in it went out there. And Noah was thankful for his deliverance, and he built an altar and offered a sacrifice to the Lord. And God set a beautiful rainbow in the sky, to show that he would never again cover the earth with water in that way. Noah lived for three hundred and fifty years after the flood, and was nine hundred and fifty years old when he died.

But it was not long before the people again forgot all about God, and their minds were filled with their own vain imaginations. As they journeyed from the east they came to a plain in the land of Shinar: and they said one to another, Come, let us build a tower that shall reach up to heaven! And they began to build a large tower of brick. But God saw their work and the wicked thoughts in their hearts, and was angry because of the building of this tower. They built it, very likely, to escape from any flood which might come again upon the earth, although God had said to Noah that there would never be such a flood again. Now at that time the people all spoke one language. So God made all those who were working at the tower each to speak a different language; and as they could not understand one another they had to stop the building. So this tower was called the Tower of Babel, because babel means confusion. This Babel, or Babylon, as it was afterwards called, was the beginning of Nimrod's kingdom in the plain of Shinar. When the people were scattered by the confusion of tongues we read that Asshur went forth and built Nineveh.

NOAH LEAVING THE ARK

Many years after these things happened there lived in the land of Ur of the Chaldees a man called Abram, a son of Terah, a descendant of Shem, one of Noah's sons. He feared God, and because the people round about him worshipped idols, God told him to go up into a country which he would show him, promising to bless him, and make of him a great nation. And Abram believed God, and departed with his wife Sarai, and Lot, his brother's son. And they came to Shechem in Canaan, where God spoke to him and told him that he would give all the land to his descendants. When a famine arose in the land, Abram had to go down to Egypt to get food; and at another time, his flocks and herds had increased so much that he had to part from Lot. And Lot, being selfish, chose the plain of Jordan, because it was rich and well-watered. But Lot was not long there, among the wicked people of Sodom, before he fell into trouble. Four kings with an army came up against Sodom and took it, and Lot and his family were amongst the captives. But Abram came and rescued Lot from these kings, and took back all the spoil which they had carried off with them. And as Abram was returning he was met by Melchizedek, king of Salem and a minister of God, who blessed him and thanked God for giving him the victory.

After this God talked with Abram. He promised him that he would have a son, and that his descendants would be like the stars for number, but that they would be strangers in a strange land, and be servants, and be ill-treated for a season. After four hundred years they would come out of that land

THE DESTRUCTION OF SODOM

with great wealth. And God changed Abram's name to Abraham, which signifies the father of many nations; and Sarai's was changed to Sarah, which means princess.

One day Abraham was seated at his tent door, in the heat of the day, when he saw three men standing near him. And he ran and bowed down before them, as is the custom in the east, and asked them to rest under a tree. Now two of these men were angels, and one of them was the Lord, although Abraham knew not this at the time. And Abraham was very kind to them, and entertained them with the best food he had; and after that they went together towards the city of Sodom.

It was now revealed to Abraham that the cities of Sodom and Gomorrah in the plain of Jordan were to be destroyed because they were so wicked. Abraham pleaded with God that if there were found a certain number of righteous men in Sodom he would not destroy it. But there were not even ten righteous people found there. And Abraham was sorry when he heard this, because Lot dwelt in Sodom. But God sent two angels to warn Lot of what was coming; and Lot told some of his friends of the great destruction impending; but they would not believe it, and only laughed at him. And the two angels hurried Lot and his wife and his two daughters out of the doomed city, and told them to depart quickly, and not look behind, else they would perish with it. And Lot fled to a city called Zoar; but on the way thither his wife looked back, and because of her disobedience she at once became a pillar of salt. And the Lord rained fire and brimstone down upon Sodom and Gomorrah, and they were destroyed, and only Lot and his daughters were saved alive.

When Abraham was about one hundred years old, God remembered his promise, and a son was born to him, whom he called Isaac. When Isaac grew up, young Ishmael, the son of Hagar, who lived in the tents with them, mocked at Isaac, and Abraham was obliged to send away Hagar and Ishmael. He gave them some bread and water for the journey; but after Hagar had been some time in the wilderness, the water was exhausted, and poor Ishmael was like to die. And Hagar wept bitterly; but God heard her cry, and showed her a well of water, and their lives were saved. As Ishmael grew up he became expert in the use of the bow and arrow, and became the father of the wandering tribes of the eastern desert.

And one day God spoke to Abraham, and asked him to do a very hard and bitter thing, that he might see if he trusted him with all his heart. He commanded Abraham to take his only and beloved son Isaac, and go into the land of Moriah, and offer him as a sacrifice upon an altar; so Abraham started early one morning, and saddled his ass, and took Isaac, and two young men who were his servants, and wood ready to lay upon the altar. On the third day he came to the place; and Abraham and Isaac went up to the mountain-top alone, and Isaac said, My father, behold the fire and the wood, but where is the lamb for a burnt offering? Abraham replied, My son, God will provide himself a lamb for a burnt-offering. And Abraham built an altar and laid the wood upon it. And then he bound Isaac, and laid him upon the wood, and took his knife to slay his son. But the angel of the Lord stayed his hand; and looking round Abraham saw a ram caught fast in the bushes by the horns; and he offered up the ram instead of Isaac.

God was now well pleased with Abraham because of his obedience and faith, as shown by his willingness to offer up his son, and he received the promise of great blessings. His descendants were to be like the sand on the sea-shore for multitude; and all nations of the earth were to be blessed in them, because the Saviour who had been promised was to be born amongst them.

CHAPTER II

THE MARRIAGE OF ISAAC—ESAU AND JACOB—JOSEPH SOLD INTO EGYPT—HE BECOMES RULER THERE—THE CHILDREN OF ISRAEL GO DOWN TO EGYPT—THE DEATH OF JOSEPH.

WHEN Isaac grew up, Abraham wished him to take a wife, but not one of the women of the country, because they were idolaters. So he sent his faithful servant to some of his own kindred, with ten camels and many beautiful presents. And when the servant came near to a city in the country to which he was sent, he brought his camels to a well, and prayed that God would show kindness to his master, and that the woman who gave him water to

ABRAHAM AND ISAAC

drink out of her pitcher when he asked it might be the wife of Isaac.

And a beautiful young woman, named Rebekah, came down to draw water with her pitcher, and the servant ran and asked for some water for himself and the camels. And she behaved kindly towards him, and drew water for him; and the servant knew at once that this was the woman that God had chosen to be Isaac's wife. And after Abraham's servant had given her some presents, he heard that she was a relation of his master's; and Laban, her brother, came out to meet him, and entertained him. Then the servant delivered his message, and told them of Abraham's wealth in camels, and oxen, and sheep, and how he wished a wife for his son. And Rebekah's friends saw that God had guided Abraham's servant thither; and the next day he started on his homeward journey, with Rebekah and her maid on the camels beside him. When they reached the land of Canaan it was towards evening, and Isaac, who had gone out to the fields to meditate, met them. And Rebekah went home with him, and became his wife, and he loved her very much.

And when Abraham was one hundred and seventy-five years old he died; and they buried him beside Sarah, in the field which he had bought from Ephron the Hittite.

And God gave Isaac two sons; the name of the eldest was Esau, and that of the youngest Jacob. Esau was a great hunter, and often brought home deer, and made food that his father loved. Jacob was a plain shepherd, living in a tent. One day Esau came in from the fields faint with hunger, and

ISAAC BLESSING ESAU

he saw Jacob cooking a mess of pottage, and he asked for some. Now Jacob was very mean, and he asked Esau for his birthright, or all that he was entitled to as the eldest son, in exchange for the pottage. And Esau consented to the exchange, and thus despised his birthright.

And a great famine arose in the land of Canaan, which caused Isaac to remove with his family and his flocks and herds to the land of Gerar. And God prospered him there, and he became very wealthy, and had great flocks of sheep, cattle and many servants. And Isaac dug again the wells of his father Abraham which had been stopped up. And God appeared to him at Beersheba, and promised to bless him.

When Isaac grew old and could not see, he sent Esau out to the field to bring home the kind of flesh that he loved, because he purposed to give Esau his blessing before he died. But Rebekah heard this; and as she loved Jacob best, she disguised him with skins, to make him hairy like Esau, so that Isaac would not know it was Jacob. And she gave him the flesh of a kid that had been newly killed, and sent him to get the blessing from his father. And Isaac blessed Jacob with the first and best blessing, as the elder son, and prayed that God would bless him with the good things of the earth, and that he might become great, and that other nations might bow down to him. When Esau came home, and found out what his brother had done, he cried out with a loud voice for his father to bless him also. And Isaac blessed him also, but not with the same great blessing as Jacob. And Esau hated

JACOB'S DREAM

Jacob for this, and purposed in his heart to kill him when he had an opportunity.

And Rebekah warned Jacob of his brother Esau's intention to kill him; so Jacob went to Padan-aram, where his uncle Laban lived. When on his journey he lighted upon a certain place, where he tarried all night, and lay down with stones for his pillow. And as he slept he dreamed that he saw a ladder set up on the earth, the top of which reached to heaven, and behold, the angels of God ascending and descending upon it. And above it stood the Lord, who made him the gracious promise that he would keep him in all the way he had to go, and give him the land wherein he was to himself and his children for a possession. In the morning Jacob took his stone pillow and poured oil upon the top of it, and called the place Bethel, which means the house of God. And he vowed that if God would be with him and keep him, the Lord should be his God.

And Jacob went on his journey until he came to Haran, where his uncle Laban lived. And near a well in a field he met Rachel, the daughter of Laban, to whom he made himself known, and assisted her in watering her sheep. Laban welcomed Jacob, and made an agreement with him, whereby if he served him seven years he would have his younger daughter Rachel, whom Jacob loved, to be his wife. But at the end of seven years, when Jacob claimed Rachel as his wife, the crafty Laban gave him her sister Leah instead, whom he did not love, and said he must serve him another seven years for Rachel. And Jacob, for the love he bore to Rachel, consented to serve another seven years for her.

Then Jacob returned to the land of Canaan, having now eleven sons and one daughter, and a great many sheep and cattle, for God had fulfilled his promise and blessed him. On the journey, at a certain place, the Lord wrestled with him for a whole night, and gave him a new name. Instead of Jacob he was to be called Israel, which means "A Prince of God." And he called the place Peniel, which means "the face of God," because he had seen God face to face. On the journey he also met his brother Esau, and they were reconciled to one another. But his wife Rachel died by the way, when his youngest son Benjamin was born. Soon after Jacob's return to Canaan his father Isaac also died. And as the land was not able to support him and Esau, to whom he was now reconciled, because of the multitude of their sheep and cattle, they parted company, and Esau dwelt in Mount Seir.

Of all his twelve sons Jacob loved Joseph best, and he made him a coat of many colors. When Joseph was about seventeen years of age, he had a strange dream, which he told to his brothers. He thought in his dream that they were all binding sheaves in the field, when his sheaf arose and stood upright, and all his brothers' sheaves stood up and bowed down to it. This caused his brothers to be very envious and jealous of him. Joseph dreamed again that the sun, the moon and eleven stars bowed down to him. All this seemed as if they, his elder brethren, who were older and wiser than him, were to bow down and serve him.

While his brethren were feeding their flocks at Shechem Joseph was sent by his father from

Hebron to see as to their welfare, and to bring him word. He found them at Dothan, about twelve miles from Shechem. When his brethren saw him afar off they made a plot against him to kill him. They could not bear his dreams, his reproofs, his airs of superiority, as they deemed them, any longer. They thought they had now a good opportunity to kill him, cast his body into a pit, and then report that some evil beast had devoured him. Reuben, his eldest brother, was a little less heartless than the rest, and begged that they would not kill him, but leave him in a pit in the wilderness. So they stripped him of his coat of many colors, and cast him into a pit, where he might have perished; but a band of merchants, Ishmaelites and Midianites, bound for the land of Egypt, coming that way, his brethren sold him to them as a slave for twenty pieces of silver. When Reuben, who did not know of this, came to the pit and found his brother Joseph gone, he was in great distress, and wondered what he should say to his father on his return. So these wicked brethren killed a kid, dipped Joseph's coat in the blood, and taking it to their father, made him believe that some evil beast had devoured him. Jacob mourned long and bitterly for his son, and said, "I will go down into the grave unto my son mourning."

Meanwhile Joseph was sold by the Ishmaelites as a slave to Potiphar, an officer of King Pharaoh, captain of his guard, who, finding him honest and diligent, trusted him, and promoted him in his service. But the wife of Potiphar was not a good woman, and made her husband believe that he had a bad ser-

JOSEPH INTERPRETS PHARAOH'S DREAM

vant, and bore false witness against him. So Joseph was sent to prison because of what this woman said against him. In prison he was kindly treated by the jailer, and interpreted the dreams of two of the king's servants, the chief butler and the chief baker, who were also in prison. The interpretation of the dreams which God gave to Joseph came exactly true: as Joseph foretold, the chief baker was hanged by Pharaoh within three days, but the chief butler was again restored to favor.

King Pharaoh had also strange dreams, which none of all the wise men in his kingdom could interpret. Then the chief butler, who had previously forgotten all about Joseph, remembered that the young Hebrew in prison had interpreted his dream correctly. So he told Pharaoh about him, and the king then sent for Joseph, and told one of his dreams to him. He thought that he was standing on the bank of the river Nile, when seven fat kine came up out of the water, and fed in a meadow. After them came seven lean kine, which swallowed up the fat ones, without making them look any better. His other dream was of seven good and full ears of corn growing on one stalk, which were swallowed up by seven poor, thin, withered ears, blasted by the east wind. Joseph explained to Pharaoh that it was God who enabled him to interpret dreams, and told him that his dreams were warnings sent by God of a great calamity which was coming upon the land. The seven fat kine and the seven good ears symbolized seven years of plenty; and the seven lean kine and seven blasted ears meant seven years of famine which were to follow. So Joseph advised the king that

THE MEETING OF JOSEPH AND BENJAMIN

during the years of plenty he should lay up in store against the years of famine, and set a wise man over the land to collect stores of food, so that the people might not perish with hunger during the years of dearth. Pharaoh saw the wisdom of this advice, and also that there was no one more fit and proper to set over the land to gather food than Joseph. So he appointed him to this post, put his own ring on his hand, gave him a gold chain and rich clothing, and a chariot to ride in, with people marching before, telling them to do him honor. Thus the youth who had been sold as a slave was proclaimed ruler over the land; only in the throne was Pharaoh greater than Joseph.

What Joseph had foretold came exactly to pass. There came seven years of plenty, and during those years Joseph gathered the corn into storehouses, and kept it till the seven years of famine. Then the people came from far and near into Egypt to buy corn, and amongst those who came were Joseph's ten brethren. When they were brought into Joseph's presence they bowed themselves to the ground before him. He recognized them at once, but spoke roughly to them, and asked them many questions, accusing them of being spies, and ordered that one of them should be detained until Benjamin, their youngest brother, had been brought to him. When they heard this their hearts reproved them, and they felt that this had come upon them because of their conduct towards Joseph. Then Joseph ordered that their sacks should be filled with corn, and each man's money restored into his sack.

And when they returned they told their father

Jacob all that the ruler in Egypt had said and done to them; also that they need not go back again to purchase corn unless they took their brother Benjamin with them. Jacob was very unhappy at the prospect of losing his well-beloved Benjamin. He said, My son shall not go down with you; for his brother is dead, and he is left alone; if mischief befall him by the way in the which ye go, then shall ye bring down my gray hairs with sorrow to the grave.

But as the famine was sore, he ordered them to take down a present of the best fruits of the land to the ruler in Egypt, and so endeavor to gain favor with him. When Joseph saw them come with Benjamin, he ordered his steward to prepare a meal, as these men were to dine with him at noon. Joseph again asked them many questions about the welfare of his father; and when he saw Benjamin with them his heart yearned over him, and he went into his chamber and wept. After that they all feasted together, and at Joseph's command the sacks of his brethren were filled with corn, the money they had brought was put back into their sacks' mouth, and Joseph's silver cup was put into Benjamin's sack. Next day, before they had got very far from the city, a messenger from Joseph stopped them and accused them of stealing his master's silver cup. They all protested that they knew nothing about it; but in spite of what they said, when their sacks were opened and examined, the cup was found in that of Benjamin. So they were obliged to go back to the ruler of Egypt, and explain the matter. Joseph said that he would detain Benjamin as his servant for what he had done. Judah, his brother, made an earnest appeal that he should be detained instead of Benjamin, for his aged father's sake.

At this Joseph could not contain himself any longer; so he made himself known to his brethren, and he wept aloud with them, so that all the house of Pharaoh heard. He said, I am Joseph; doth my father yet live? None of them could answer him, for they were afraid. But Joseph calmed their fears, and told them that although they had sold him as a slave into Egypt, God had sent him before them to preserve their lives. And he requested them to go at once to the land of Canaan, and bring their father, and their families, and all their flocks and herds, and he would make abundant provision for them all in the land of Goshen. And this pleased Pharaoh also, and he promised them the good of all the land of Egypt.

And Jacob began his journey, and at Beersheba he offered sacrifices to the God of his father. And God appeared to him in a dream, and told him not to be afraid to go down into the land of Egypt, for the Lord would be with him, and make of him a great nation.

When Jacob came down into Egypt he was presented to Pharaoh, and blessed him; and Joseph gave his father and brethren a possession in the land of Egypt, in the country of Goshen, and he fed them with bread during all the years of famine.

After living for seventeen years in Egypt, the time came when Jacob must die. He blessed the two sons of Joseph, Ephraim and Manasseh; and told Joseph that although he was now passing away, God would be with his posterity and bring them again into the land of Canaan. Then he blessed his twelve sons, foretelling what they and their descendants would become. Judah received the highest honor, for his descendants were declared to be the royal tribe, which would never be without a ruler until Shiloh should come, and unto him should the gathering of the people be. After Joseph and Benjamin had received a very tender blessing, he commanded them to bury him in the land of Canaan, in the cave, in the field of Machpelah, which had been Abraham's burying-place. When Jacob died his body was embalmed, or preserved with spices; and after seventy days the children of Israel went up with chariots and horsemen, a very great company, and buried him in the cave of Machpelah, as he had commanded.

After the death of their father, the sons of Jacob were afraid that Joseph would now punish them for their former cruel behavior to him in selling him as a slave. When they confessed to him their fears, and that they had done wrong, and had asked his forgiveness, Joseph wept, and told them that though they had sold him into Egypt, and had intended to do him harm, God had turned it into good. So he comforted and spoke kindly to them, and assured them that he would provide for their households. When Joseph came to die, he told the children of Israel (as Jacob's descendants were henceforth called) that God would surely visit them, and bring them up into the land of Canaan. He also made them promise to carry his bones with them and lay them there.

CHAPTER III

THE OPPRESSION IN EGYPT—THE BIRTH OF MOSES— HE IS APPOINTED DELIVERER—THE PLAGUES OF EGYPT—PHARAOH LETS THE PEOPLE GO.

MANY years after the death of Joseph and the good Pharaoh who had made him ruler in the land there rose up a king who knew not Joseph. This Pharaoh had become jealous of the growing wealth and greatness of the children of Israel in the land of Goshen, and he thought he would try and keep them down, in case, if there came war with a neighboring country, they might join his enemies. So he began to treat them like slaves; he set hard taskmasters over them, and made them make bricks and build treasure-houses for him —Pithom and Raamses. And he not only did this, but he ordered that all the Hebrew boys should be destroyed at their birth, thinking that in this way he would stop the increase of the Israelites in the land. There was one tender-hearted Hebrew mother who managed to hide her babe out of sight for three months, until she could hide him no longer. So she made a cradle of water-reeds, and daubed it with pitch that it might not sink when put into the water, and then she placed it among the rushes at the edge of the river Nile. After a time it so happened that Pharaoh's daughter, coming down to the river to bathe, saw the cradle with the babe in it, and sent her maid to fetch it. The child cried as she looked at him, and taking pity upon him she ordered that

THE FINDING OF MOSES

the little foundling should be nursed for her by a Hebrew woman. And Miriam, the sister of the child, who had been standing afar off, went and fetched his own mother as nurse for him. And she nursed him for Pharaoh's daughter, and he was named Moses, which means "drawn out," because he had been drawn out of the water.

The princess gave him the best education that could be had at that time; and he became learned in in all the wisdom of the Egyptians. But although brought up at the court of Pharaoh he did not forget his own people. When he was forty years of age his spirit was stirred within him one day by seeing an Egyptian ill-treating one of his own nation. He took the part of the Hebrew, and slew the Egyptian, and buried his body in the sand. Next day, when he interfered again in another quarrel, he found that what he had done the day before was known, and he fled into the land of Midian.

One day, as Moses sat beside a well in Midian, seven maidens came out with their father's sheep to water them, but could not do so because of the shepherds there who tried to drive them away. Moses took their part, and helped them to water their sheep; and when the maidens went home they told their father that they had been helped by a stranger. So Moses was invited into the house of Jethro, and treated kindly, and he married one of Jethro's daughters, called Zipporah. These Midianites were related to the children of Israel, for they were descended from Midian, a son of Abraham, who had gone to live in the eastward of the land of Canaan.

Moses lived quietly in Midian for about forty years

as a shepherd, in gradual preparation for the great work which lay before him. During this time the afflictions of the Israelites in Egypt increased. It had been revealed to Abraham that they would have to endure this cruel bondage for about four hundred years, and then a deliverer would arise.

One day Moses was feeding his flock on the mountain of Horeb when he saw a bush burning with fire, yet not consumed. He turned aside to see this strange sight, when a voice called him by name out of the middle of the bush. He was told to put his shoes from off his feet, for the ground on which he stood was holy. It was God who spoke, and Moses hid his face, for he was afraid to look upon God. Then God told him how he had heard the cry and seen the affliction of his people in Egypt, and that he wished him to go to Pharaoh and ask him to let his people go.

Moses did not think he was worthy to do this great work, and asked for a proof to give to his brethren that he was sent by God. He was told to say to them, I AM—which means the same as Jehovah, the everlasting God—hath sent me unto you. He was first to call together the chief men of Israel, and then go to Pharaoh, and ask leave for the children of Israel to go three days' journey into the wilderness to sacrifice to God. And in order that the people might not doubt his word he was given the power of working miracles. The rod which he held in his hand when cast to the ground became a serpent, and when he took hold of it again it became a rod. And also, when he put his hand into his bosom and took it out, it was covered with a terrible disease called leprosy; when he put it back again and took it not it became as whole as the other. Still Moses did not think he was quite equal to the task, because he was slow of speech; but God reproved him, and said, Now, therefore, go, and I will be with thy mouth, and teach thee what thou shalt say. Further, he was commanded to take his brother Aaron with him, who was ready and fluent of speech, and who would be his spokesman to the people.

The first interview which Moses and Aaron had with Pharaoh seemed only to make the case of the people worse than before. Their taskmasters behaved more cruelly to them, and did not even give them straw to make bricks, but told them they might seek straw for themselves. And Moses cried to God, and in answer he was encouraged not to be afraid, for God would not forsake his people in their trouble, but would certainly remember his promise, and bring them safely into the land of Canaan. But the people were now so down-trodden and miserable, that they would scarcely believe that his promise would ever be fulfilled.

And Moses and Aaron, by God's command, went a second time to the king; and Aaron threw down his rod before him, and it became a serpent. But the conjurors or magicians of the court made Pharaoh believe that they could do the same thing; and they also threw down their rods, which became serpents, but Aaron's rod swallowed theirs up. All this had no effect upon the mind of the king, who still hardened his heart.

God now commanded Moses and Aaron to go to the brink of the Nile when the king came there in the morning, and Aaron was to stretch forth his rod over the waters of Egypt, and immediately they would be changed into blood, and the river would stink, and all the fish that were in it would die. Moses and Aaron obeyed the command, and all the rivers of Egypt were at once changed into blood. And the magicians did so, or appeared to do so, with their enchantments, and the heart of Pharaoh remained as hard as ever.

When seven days had expired, Moses went again to the king to ask that the children of Israel might be allowed to go, and told him that if he again refused the land would be visited with a plague of frogs. So when Aaron stretched his hand over the waters of Egypt, the frogs came up and covered the land. This plague was so troublesome that Pharaoh in distress sent for Moses and Aaron, and asked them to take away the frogs; so on the morrow Moses cried unto the Lord, and the plague of frogs was confined to the river. When Pharaoh saw that there was to be a respite, he again hardened his heart, and would not let the people go.

The next plague sent on Pharaoh for his hardness of heart was that the dust of the earth became lice both on man and beast; but this also had no effect upon the heart of the king. Then a plague of flies was sent, which filled the houses of the Egyptians, so that the land was perfectly corrupted by them. Pharaoh relented again, and was willing to let them go until the plague was removed, when his heart remained as hard as ever. Next, disease was sent upon the cattle of the Egyptians, then grievous boils were sent upon man and beast, and thunder and hail, which worked havoc amongst the cattle and in the fields of the Egyptians. The next two plagues were locusts and darkness. But the heart of the king remained as hard as before until the last and most terrible plague of all, when all the first-born of man and beast were slain throughout the land. God had warned Moses that after this Pharaoh would let the children of Israel go.

CHAPTER IV

THE PASSOVER APPOINTED—THE FIRST-BORN OF THE EGYPTIANS SLAIN—THE CHILDREN OF ISRAEL DEPART—THE PASSAGE OF THE RED SEA—THE GIVING OF THE LAW—THE PLAN OF THE TABERNACLE—FEASTS APPOINTED.

SOME preparation was needed before the children of Israel should leave the land in which they had now lived for about four hundred and thirty years. They were therefore commanded to borrow of the Egyptians jewels of silver and jewels of gold, and all other things necessary; and in memory of their deliverance they were to celebrate the Lord's Passover; an ordinance which was to be kept up through all their generations. A lamb was to be killed and roasted during the night, and eaten with unleavened bread and bitter herbs. And they were to take of the blood and strike it on the two side-posts and the upper post of the doors of the houses in which they were eating it. The flesh of the lamb was to be eaten with their loins girded, their shoes on their feet, and their staff in their hand. From the fourteenth day of the month until the twenty-first nothing but unleavened bread was to be found in any of their houses; and when the Lord would pass through to smite the first-born of the Egyptians all the doors, where the lintels and side-posts were sprinkled with blood, would be *passed over*.

What the Lord had revealed to Moses came to pass. All the first-born in the land of Egypt, from Pharaoh on the throne to the captive in the dungeon, were smitten, as well as the first-born of cattle. A great cry was raised during the night, such as there had not been before nor since, when Pharaoh and the Egyptians discovered this terrible calamity. Moses and Aaron were at once sent for, and commanded to lead the children of Israel forth, for they said, We be all dead men. And the Lord gave them favor in the eyes of the Egyptians, so that they lent to the people jewels of silver and jewels of gold, and all that they required from them. And they departed in haste, a vast multitude, on foot. They first journeyed from Rameses to Succoth; and from thence they marched to Etham, on the edge of the wilderness. They had a sign that the Lord was leading them in a pillar of cloud which hung over them by day, but which became a pillar of fire at night, going before them to show the way.

The heart of Pharaoh was not long in turning against the children of Israel after he had let them go, especially when it was told him that they were fleeing from him. The Egyptians felt annoyed that they had allowed them to go away from serving them. So with their horses and chariots they pursued them, and came close to them beside Pihahiroth. The sight of their oppressors pursuing them caused the Israelites to become faint-hearted and tremble, and also to murmur against Moses for leading them out thus to perish in the wilderness. Moses laid their trouble before the Lord, and the answer came, Speak to the children of Israel that they go forward. And the angel of God went from the front to the rear of the children of Israel, and the pillar of cloud hung behind them, between them and their enemies. And Moses at God's command stretched his rod over the waters of the Red Sea, and the waters went back all that night by a strong east wind, making the sea dry land, and the waters were divided. Into this pathway made for them in the waters the children of Israel marched, with a wall of water on their right hand and on their left, closely pursued by the Egyptians, who went in after them even to the midst of the sea.

And the Lord looked down upon the Egyptians and troubled them, and commanded Moses to stretch his hand over the sea, and when he had done so, the sea returned in its strength, and all the Egyptians with their chariots and horsemen were swallowed up in the waters; but the children of Israel marched safely over upon dry land. And on the other side Moses and the whole congregation of Israel sang a song of triumph unto the Lord about the overthrow of their enemies. And Miriam, the prophetess, the sister of Moses, took a timbrel in her hand, and followed by the women, she said, Sing ye to the

THE ISRAELITES PASSING THROUGH THE RED SEA

Lord, for he hath triumphed gloriously: the horse and his rider hath he thrown into the sea.

From the Red Sea they marched to the wilderness of Shur, where they wandered three days without finding water. Then they came to Marah, but the water there was so bitter that until Moses, at the command of the Lord, had cast a certain tree in it they could not drink. And here the promise of God came to them, that if they would hearken diligently to his voice, and do right in his sight, and keep his commandments, they would never be visited with the plagues which they had seen come upon the Egyptians.

When they came to the wilderness of Sin, the people again began to murmur against Moses, and to long for the flesh-pots of Egypt which they had left behind them. They accused him of having brought them into the wilderness to perish of hunger.

Then the word of the Lord came to Moses that the murmurings of the people had been heard, and that their wants were to be supplied in a miraculous way. In the evening a flight of quails came up and covered the camp, and the people gathered sufficient of them to supply their needs. In the morning, after the dew had gone up from the earth, a small round thing, as small as the hoar-frost, lay upon the ground. Moses told the people that this was the bread which God had provided for them, and they called it manna, which means, "What is this?" They were to gather a certain quantity every morning; and when the sun grew hot the manna melted away. And if they kept it till next morning it bred worms and stank. On the sixth day they gathered a double quantity, as much as would last them over the seventh day, which was to be for them a day of rest. During all the forty years in which the children of Israel wandered in the desert they were fed with this manna, until they came unto the borders of the land of Canaan.

The people again journeyed onward until they came to Rephidim. Here there was no water, and they were again angry at Moses, and were ready to kill him by casting stones at him. At the command of God Moses went with the chief men to the rock in Horeb, and struck the rock with his rod, and the waters gushed out and ran in the dry places like a river. Moses called the place Massah, or "temptation," because the people had tempted the Lord to anger by their complainings, and Meribah, or "strife," because of their threatenings against Moses.

Another trouble now came upon them. A powerful tribe, descended from Duke Amalek, one of the grandsons of Esau, seeing such a host in the valley of Rephidim, came up behind them, and attacked the most defenceless of the host of Israel. Moses bade a young man named Joshua go forth and fight against them with a chosen band of men. He then ascended a hill near at hand, with Aaron and Hur, and when he held up his hand with his rod in it, Joshua had the best of the fight, but whenever he let down his hand through weariness then Amalek prevailed. When Moses grew weary in holding up his hands, a stone was placed for him upon which to sit, while Aaron and Hur stood, one on each side of him, and held up his hands. This continued until sunset, when Joshua had won the battle. A record of this fight was commanded to be kept, so that it could be read by future generations that they might know how God fought for them, and how they prevailed. Moses also built an altar, and called it Jehovah-nissi, "The Lord my Banner."

Shortly after this great event Moses was visited by Jethro his father-in-law, who brought with him his daughter Zipporah, the wife of Moses, with her two sons, Gershom and Eliezer, who had remained behind in Midian for safety. Moses welcomed them, and told Jethro of the wonders which the Lord had wrought for them, which made his father-in-law rejoice, and say, Now I know that the Lord is greater than all gods. At that time Moses acted as the judge as well as the leader of the people, and he might be seen sitting all day hearing their troubles and disputes. Jethro saw that this was more than the strength of Moses could bear, and suggested that able men, who feared God and could be trusted, should be set over the people to judge them. This was done, and Moses was relieved of an arduous duty, only the hard causes being brought before him.

After the children of Israel departed from Rephidim they came to the desert of Sinai, and encamped there. From the top of Mount Sinai God spoke to the people in a thick cloud, with thunders and lightnings and the voice of a trumpet, so that all the people trembled. The mount seemed altogether on a smoke, for the Lord descended upon it in fire. Moses was called up to the top of the mount with Aaron, while the people waited below, and the Lord

MOSES AND THE TEN COMMANDMENTS

delivered to them the commandments which were to be kept by themselves and their children. Unto Moses, Aaron, Nadab and Abihu, and seventy of the elders of Israel, was the vision of the glory of the God of Israel given. And again Moses was called up into the mount, and remained beneath the shadow of the cloud forty days and forty nights, until the Lord had delivered to him the plan of the tabernacle, and all its furniture, which he was to build for the worship of the one true God.

When Moses was absent from the camp on Mount Sinai, the people at the foot of the mount grew impatient of his return, and complained to Aaron, and asked him to make them idols, such as were worshipped by heathen nations, for as for this Moses they did not know what had become of him. So Aaron asked them to bring their jewels of gold, and these he melted, and made into a golden calf. And when the people saw it they said this was the god which had brought them up out of the land of Egypt. And Aaron built an altar before it, and offered sacrifice to it instead of to the Lord, and there was a great feast, and the people danced before the calf.

And God told Moses while on the mount what the people were doing in his absence; and he hastened down from the mount, and as he drew near with Joshua, he heard the noise of singing and dancing in the camp. Moses was so angry when he saw the people dancing before the golden calf that he threw the two tables of stone out of his hand upon which the commandments were written, and they were broken in pieces. And Moses took the calf, and burned it with fire, and ground it into dust, and strewed it amongst water, and made the children of Israel drink of this water. Then Moses stood at the gate of the camp and asked all those who were on the Lord's side to come beside him. Then the children of Levi came to him, and he commanded them to go through the camp and slay every man they should meet, because of their great sin in worshipping the golden calf. And Moses prayed to God for the people, and confessed their sin, and asked forgiveness for them.

After this Moses was commanded by God to make two tables of stone like to those which he had broken, and early in the morning he went up to the top of Mount Sinai alone, and again interceded in prayer for the sins of the people. And God heard him, and took them to be his people again; and he commanded Moses to write on the two tables of stone the words of the ten commandments as follows:

I. Thou shalt have none other gods but me.

II. Thou shalt not make to thyself any graven image, nor the likeness of any thing that is in heaven above, or in the earth beneath, or in the water under the earth. Thou shalt not bow down to them, nor worship them : for I the Lord thy God am a jealous God, and visit the sins of the fathers upon the children, unto the third and fourth generation of them that hate me, and show mercy unto thousands of them that love me, and keep my commandments.

III. Thou shalt not take the name of the Lord thy God in vain: for the Lord will not hold him guiltless that taketh his name in vain.

IV. Remember that thou keep holy the Sabbath

day. Six days shalt thou labor, and do all that thou hast to do; but the seventh day is the Sabbath of the Lord thy God. In it thou shalt do no manner of work, thou, and thy son and thy daughter, thy man-servant, and thy maid-servant, thy cattle, and the stranger that is within thy gates. For in six days the Lord made heaven and earth, the sea, and all that in them is, and rested the seventh day: wherefore the Lord blessed the seventh day and hallowed it.

V. Honor thy father and thy mother; that thy days may be long in the land which the Lord thy God giveth thee.

VI. Thou shalt do no murder.

VII. Thou shalt not commit adultery.

VIII. Thou shalt not steal.

IX. Thou shalt not bear false witness against thy neighbor.

X. Thou shalt not covet thy neighbor's house, thou shalt not covet thy neighbor's wife, nor his servant, nor his maid, nor his ox, nor his ass, nor any thing that is his.

When Moses came down from the mount his face shone with a heavenly brightness, for he had been communing with God; and he bore the tables of stone in his hand upon which were written the commandments. Aaron and the people were afraid to speak with him until he had put a veil upon his face.

Then Moses told the people what God had commanded him to do on Mount Sinai about the building of the tabernacle; and he invited all those whose hearts were willing, to bring him suitable gifts of what they possessed, and those who were clever workmen at any special trade he also invited to assist in building the tabernacle. Before the Hebrews had left Egypt they had borrowed of the Egyptians jewels of silver and gold, and many valuable and useful things. These were now of great service, and so were the skilled workmen, who had learned to weave cloth and make useful articles during their sojourn in Egypt. And the people came, both men and women, as many as were willing-hearted, and brought gold, and precious stones, and cloth, blue, purple and scarlet, and fine linen, and goats' hair. And these offerings of the people were publicly given to the skilled workmen, Bezaleel and Aholiab, in order that they might proceed with the work for which such abundance of material had been brought.

This tabernacle, which was to be the visible sign of the presence of God with the children of Israel and their meeting-place with him, was both beautiful and costly. It was divided into two parts, the holy place and the holy of holies, which were separated from one another by a beautiful curtain called the veil. In the holy place stood the golden altar of incense, having on its north side the table of shew-bread, which consisted of twelve loaves of fine flour, and on its south side a golden candlestick. On this candlestick were seven lamps, one on each branch, ornamented with golden flowers. The lamps were kept burning constantly, only pure olive-oil being used for them. In the holy of holies stood the ark of the covenant, which was made of shittim-wood covered with gold; this ark held the tables of the law, and a golden pot filled with manna, which was to be kept through all their generations. The top of the ark, where a golden cherub with outstretched wings stood at each end, was called the mercy-seat. Here the Lord met with Moses, and talked to him from above the mercy-seat, between the cherubim.

The sides of the tabernacle were of boards covered with gold, with a curtain of many colors for a door; it stood within an enclosure, which was surrounded by pillars of brass, and hangings of fine linen of

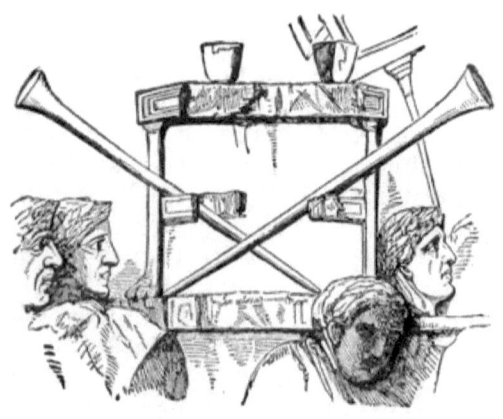

THE TABLE OF SHEW-BREAD.

many-colored needlework. In front of the tabernacle and within this court stood an altar and a laver; this altar was for burnt offerings, and the laver, which was of brass, held water in which the priests washed their hands before entering the tabernacle itself. The whole structure was so made that it could be easily carried about with the children of Israel in their desert wanderings.

STORY OF THE OLD TESTAMENT 53

Aaron was appointed high priest, and his four sons were set apart for the priest's office, to assist him; and suitable garments were made for them. For the high priest there was a breast-plate of fine twined linen and of work of many colors, folded square, in which were set twelve stones in gold, each stone bearing the name of one of the twelve tribes of

THE GOLDEN CANDLESTICK.

Israel. Then there was a garment called an ephod, for Aaron to wear, made of fine linen of many colors, which was fastened with an onyx stone to each shoulder. A robe or coat was made to be worn under the ephod, all of blue, and round its lower edge were hung pomegranates of blue and purple and scarlet, between which were golden bells, which would ring as the high priest went out and in to the tabernacle. On the mitre for Aaron's head were inscribed the words "Holiness to the Lord."

When the work of the tabernacle was finished, Moses looked over it all, and saw that it was made as God had commanded. And when it was set up, the pillar of the cloud that had gone before the children of Israel came down over the tabernacle; and the glory of the Lord filled it, so that Moses could not go within it. And so it became the place where God spoke to Moses, from the cloud over the mercy-seat.

The people were then called together for the consecration of the tabernacle to the service of the Lord. And as they stood round the door of the tabernacle, Moses washed Aaron and his sons with water, and put on them their beautiful garments, and anointed them with oil. And thus Aaron and his sons were set apart for the priesthood, to offer up sacrifices to God for the sins of the people.

The tabernacle was finished on the first day of the first month, and the seven lamps upon the golden candlestick were lighted, and sweet incense was offered upon the altar. And Aaron took a lamb, and killed it, and laid it upon the altar as an offering to God for the sins of the people. And the Lord sent fire, which burned up the lamb, and the people gave a great shout in token that the sacrifice had been accepted. After this the fire was kept burning upon the altar continually.

Moses now received commands from God as to the different kinds of sacrifice which were to be offered up, the highest kind being the burnt-sacrifice with blood. The priests were ordered to offer up a lamb in the morning and in the evening for the sins of the whole people. On the Sabbath-day two lambs and two kids were offered morning and evening. And if any man repented him of his sins, he brought an ox, or a sheep, or a goat to the door of the tabernacle. Then he put his hand upon its head, which meant that he transferred his sins to the animal; after which it was killed, and the priests burnt it upon the altar as a sacrifice to God. This was called a burnt-offering. But when a man wished to thank God especially for some blessing which he had received, or wished to ask for some blessing, the animal was only partly burned, and was eaten partly by the priests and by the man for whom the sacrifice was offered. This kind of sacrifice was called a peace-offering. Sacrifices offered for pardon of sins done in ignorance of what was right were called sin-offerings. Those for particular sins or trespasses were called trespass-offerings. The offering of any kind of meat, such as flour, oil or herbs, was called the meat and drink offering, which was burned or poured out upon the altar. The best of everything was only to be given in all these sacrifices.

Three feasts to God were also appointed to be held every year: the feast of the passover, the feast of pentecost and the feast of tabernacles. The first of these, as already explained, was in memory of the night when the Lord killed the first-born of the Egyptians but passed over the children of Israel, and of their deliverance from the house of bondage. The second was a festival for the harvest; and the last a special thanksgiving for the safe ingathering of the fruits of the earth. The feast of tabernacles lasted seven days, during which time the people dwelt in booths, in remembrance of the time when they were brought out of the land of Egypt.

There were other festivals: the festival of the Sabbath, which was a day of rest; the festival of the new moon every month; and on the first day of the seventh month the feast of trumpets, when trumpets were blown to call it to the mind of the people. The seventh or Sabbatical year was to be observed when they got to the land of Canaan, and in that year the land was allowed to rest; but to make up for this, God was to cause the sixth year to bring forth fruit for three years. The feast of jubilee was the feast of the fiftieth year; it was a year of rest, in which there was neither sowing nor reaping.

Every year there was to be a great fast, called the day of atonement; this was the only day in the year in which the high priest was to enter the holy of holies, and before he entered he was to offer sacrifices for his own sins and the sins of the people. When he came out he was to take a goat which had not been sacrificed, and lay his hands upon it, and confess the sins of the people, putting them upon the head of the animal, which was called the scapegoat. Then this animal was to be led away to the wilderness, to wander whither it would.

Some days after the consecration of the tabernacle, Nadab and Abihu, two of the newly-consecrated priests, offered incense with strange fire before the Lord, which he commanded them not. And there went out fire from the Lord and devoured them. And Moses commanded that Aaron and his family

DEATH OF THE DISOBEDIENT PRIESTS NADAB AND ABIHU

should not mourn for them. God warned the people at this time against imitating some of the heathen nations amongst whom they would sojourn, in offering up their children to a huge brass idol called Molech. This idol had the face of a calf, and was hollow inside, and a fire was lighted within it. And after the fire was lighted, and the idol was made very hot, these heathens placed their children in its arms until they were burned to death. And God told them also that if they walked in the way of his commandments he would prosper them; but he warned them that if they forgot to serve him, sickness and trouble would be sent upon them, until they turned their hearts again to him.

CHAPTER V

THE MARCH THROUGH THE WILDERNESS—MIRIAM STRUCK WITH LEPROSY—THE SPIES SENT OUT—THE REBELLION OF KORAH—THE DEATH OF AARON—THE BRAZEN SERPENT.

THE time now came for the people to leave Mount Sinai, where they had remained about a year, and continue their journey towards the land of Canaan. This had been an eventful year for them. God had communed with Moses on Sinai, and given him laws to regulate the conduct of the people, the ten commandments; also the plan of the tabernacle, which had now been built, and all the rules whereby they were to worship him by means of the tabernacle service. They were now divided into thirteen tribes, each of whom was descended from one of the sons of Jacob or of Joseph. The names of the tribes were Reuben, Simeon, Levi, Judah, Zebulun, Issachar, Dan, Gad, Asher, Naphtali, Ephraim, Manasseh and Benjamin. And the men who were able to go out to war were counted, and found to number six hundred and three thousand five hundred and fifty. But the children of Levi were not counted for war, but were set apart for the service of the tabernacle. No one save the priests and Levites was to come near or touch anything belonging to it, because it was consecrated to the service of the Lord. And the men of the tribe of Levi were appointed to take down the tabernacle, and to carry it when on their journey, and assist in the work required in connection with it when it remained in the camp. When the Levites were numbered, it was found that there were of them eight thousand five hundred and eighty men. And twelve princes from the twelve tribes brought six covered wagons and twelve oxen, along with many gold and silver articles, for use in the service of the tabernacle.

Whenever the tabernacle was set up, the pillar of cloud, which was the color of a cloud by day and of fire by night, came and stood over the tabernacle; and whenever this cloud was lifted up, the children of Israel knew it was time to start again on their journey, and whenever it stopped they stopped also. It was the visible presence of God in their midst. When the people were to be gathered together, or when they were about to march, the priests sounded two silver trumpets. When marching they carried standards or banners, each tribe moving in order, with the Levites in their midst bearing the tabernacle. When they stopped to make their camp anywhere, the tabernacle was set up in their midst, with the tents of the Levites beside it, and those of the different tribes all round it. There they remained until ready to move forward again.

At last the cloudy pillar rose from the tabernacle, and the people left Mount Sinai and followed it for three days into the wilderness of Paran. They became very discontented on this journey, and complained, Who shall give us meat to eat? We remember the fish that we had in Egypt; the cucumbers, the melons and the onions; but now our soul is dried away. This complaining caused the Lord to be displeased with them. And Moses entreated the Lord that he might be delivered from the leadership of the people; it was more than he was able to bear. And God answered Moses, and said he would send them flesh for a whole month. Moses unbelievingly doubted if all the thousands which he saw around him could be fed with flesh for that time; and the Lord reproved Moses for his want of trust in him. Then the Lord sent a wind which brought quails from the sea, and the ground around the camp was covered with them. The people gathered them in abundance, but there was no blessing with them, for a plague broke out amongst them, so that many of them died. And Moses called the place Kibroth-hattaavah, because there they buried the people that lusted for flesh.

They now journeyed to a place called Hazeroth, and there encamped. About this time Miriam, the sister of Moses and Aaron his brother, became jealous of Moses. They spoke against him because he had married a wife who did not belong to the tribes of Israel. They also said, Hath the Lord indeed spoken only by Moses? hath he not spoken also by us? And the Lord was displeased with them for this, and called Aaron and Miriam before him, and rebuked them; and Miriam was stricken with leprosy because of her sin; then Aaron was seized with remorse, and entreated Moses to intercede for them; but Miriam was shut outside the camp for seven days. Moses then prayed the Lord to heal her, and his prayer was heard.

When the Israelites had reached the wilderness of Paran they were not far from the land of Canaan, and Moses said to them, Behold the Lord thy God hath set the land before thee; go up and possess it, as the Lord God of thy fathers hath said unto thee: fear not, neither be discouraged. But the people asked that men might be sent to look at the land and report what they saw. So twelve men were chosen, one from each tribe, and amongst them were Caleb, the son of Jephunneh, and Joshua, the son of Nun.

These spies, as they were called, went forth to look at the land, and returned after forty days. To show the fruitfulness of the country, they brought away from Eshcol a bunch of grapes so large that it took two men to carry it. They also brought with them some pomegranates and figs, and said that the land was a fruitful land, but that the cities were very strong, with high walls round them. They had also seen giants, the people of Anak and the Amalekites;

and they all, except Caleb and Joshua, tried to frighten the people, and persuade them not to go up against such warlike tribes. This made the Israelites discontented, and they murmured that they would rather have died in Egypt, or in the wilderness, and they even wanted to choose a captain to lead them back.

But Caleb and Joshua advised the people to go up to Canaan, and said the land was an exceeding good land, and that God would fight for them. Whereat the people were angry, and threatened to stone them. And the Lord was displeased because of their want of faith in him, and Moses entreated the Lord in their behalf. And the Lord said to Moses that he would pardon them, but not one of the murmurers, from twenty years old and upwards, should enter the promised land, but should perish in the wilderness. After forty years, when they had passed away, their children would go up to this good land; but none would be allowed to enter into Canaan save Caleb and Joshua, because of their good report. At the command of God Moses was to lead the people back towards the wilderness by the way of the Red Sea, and they were to wander there for forty years. Some of the people thought that they might still go up to the good land, although Moses had warned them that God had forbidden them: and these headstrong people started on their journey without the ark or Moses to guide them. But they were attacked, and scattered, and killed by the Amalekites and the Canaanites, at Hormah.

Now after this time a rebellion against Moses and Aaron took place in the camp. The ringleaders were named Korah, Dathan and Abiram, and two hundred and fifty princes of Israel followed them. They said to Moses and Aaron, Ye take too much upon you, seeing all the congregation are holy. Wherefore lift ye up yourselves above the congregation?

After inquiring of the Lord what he ought to do, Moses bade Korah and his company come on the morrow with lighted censers before the tabernacle. Even to-morrow, he said, the Lord would show who were his and who were holy, and he asked them why they were not content with their present duties that they should covet the office of priest also. On the following day Korah and his company came up to the tabernacle with their censers and fire in them, and sprinkled incense on the fire just as the priests did. All those who joined in this rebellion crowded around to witness what the result would be. And the Lord told Moses to warn the people, and he said, Separate yourselves from among this congregation, that I may consume them in a moment. Moses prayed for them, and the Lord warned the people to separate themselves from the evil-doers, lest they should be destroyed along with them. If they died a strange death, then all the people would know that the anger of the Lord had been kindled against them.

When Moses had done warning the people, the earth suddenly opened and swallowed up Korah, Dathan and Abiram, and all who were with them. They went down alive, crying out; and all the people, in terror at this judgment of God, fled from the place, in case the same calamity should overtake them also.

And fire went forth from the Lord and consumed the two hundred and fifty princes who had followed Korah.

Next day the people seemed to have entirely forgotten the lesson they had just received, for they murmured against Moses and Aaron, saying, Ye have killed the people of the Lord. And the Lord sent forth a plague by which fourteen thousand and seven hundred persons perished, besides Korah and they that perished with him.

In order to show the people whom he had chosen to be his high priest, God commanded Moses to ask a man of each of the twelve tribes to bring a rod, which was to be placed in the holy of holies before the ark. On each rod the name of the person who brought it was written. Next day one of the rods had blossomed and borne almonds; this was the rod upon which was Aaron's name. This rod God commanded Moses to put back into the tabernacle again, to be kept as a perpetual memorial of his choice of Aaron and his descendants to the office of high priest. Then the Lord gave instructions as to the position of the tribe of Levi in the work of the tabernacle, and warned them against the sin of Korah, Dathan and Abiram, and ordered what proportion of the offerings of the people should belong to them and to the priests. The tribe of Levi when they came to the promised land were not to have any portion of the country allotted to them, because the Lord was to be their portion, and hence the people must make some provision for them.

When we next get a glimpse of the life of the children of Israel in the desert, we find that they had wandered there about thirty-eight years, being fed with manna from the Lord, and so cared for by him that they were never footsore, neither did their clothes wear out. They again arrived near the place where they had murmured at first on their journey, and came to the desert of Zin, where Miriam, the sister of Moses, died and was buried. Although those who had sinned by murmuring before were nearly all dead, yet we find the people again discontented. They began to say that they would rather have died with their brethren in the wilderness, for the place they were now in yielded neither seed, nor figs, nor vines, nor pomegranates, neither was there any water to drink.

And Moses and Aaron went to the Lord with the complaint of the people, and the Lord spoke to Moses, and told him to take his rod, and gather the assembly of the people together, and speak to the rock, and water would flow from it. And when the congregation of the people was gathered together, Moses and Aaron spoke angrily to them and said, Hear now, ye rebels; must we fetch you water out of the rock? And Moses smote the rock twice, and water flowed forth abundantly, and there was plenty for man and beast. But the Lord was displeased with Moses and Aaron because they had not sanctified him before the congregation of the people, therefore he told them they would not be honored to lead the people into the land of promise.

And they journeyed to Mount Hor, where the word of the Lord came that Aaron was to die. And Aaron and Eleazar, his son, went up with Moses to Mount Hor, and Aaron was stripped of his priestly garments, and they were put upon his son, who succeeded him in his office. And Aaron died there, and the people mourned for him thirty days.

As they journeyed from Mount Hor by way of the Red Sea, the people were so much discouraged because of the way that they murmured against Moses again. And the Lord sent fiery serpents among them, which bit them, so that many of them died. Then the people confessed to Moses that they had sinned in murmuring, and asked him to entreat the Lord on their behalf. And Moses prayed for the people, and at God's command made a serpent of brass and set it upon a pole, and every one who looked at this serpent, although they were bitten, lived.

The children of Israel wished to pass on their way to Canaan in a peaceable manner if possible, and sent messengers unto Sihon, king of the Amorites, whose country they were approaching, that he would let them pass through his land. They would not meddle with his vineyards, but would pass along the highway of his country. Sihon refused this request, and sent out an army to fight against them. But Israel prevailed, and took all his cities. And Og, king of Bashan, also rose against them, but the Lord delivered him into their hands, and they smote him and all his people with the edge of the sword.

MOSES AND THE BRAZEN SERPENT

CHAPTER VI

THE BLESSING OF BALAAM—THE DEATH OF MOSES —JOSHUA APPOINTED TO BE LEADER—THE FALL OF JERICHO—THE VICTORY OVER THE FIVE KINGS —THE DEATH OF JOSHUA.

THE children of Israel now marched forward and encamped on the plains of Moab. And Balak, the king of Moab, sent a message to Balaam, son of Beor, at Pethor, asking him to come and curse the children of Israel, so that he might prevail against them. But God warned Balaam, saying, Thou shalt not go with them; thou shalt not curse the people: for they are blessed.

So Balaam rose up in the morning, and told the princes of Balak to go back, because the Lord refused to allow him to curse the people. These men delivered their message to Balak, but he sent more princes with the same message. But Balaam said that although Balak was to give him his house full of silver and gold he could not go beyond the word of the Lord to do less or more. Then the Lord told Balaam to go with the messengers and speak the word which he would tell him. So Balaam rose up in the morning, and saddled his ass, and went with them.

But God was angry because he went, and the angel of the Lord stood in his way to stop him. And the ass upon which he rode saw the angel of the Lord standing with a drawn sword in his hand, and turned out of the way into a field, and would not go straight forward. And Balaam smote the ass to make it go straight forward, and as they were in a path between two vineyards the ass swerved aside and crushed Balaam's foot against the wall, so that he smote her again. And she fell down under him, and he smote the ass with a staff. And God gave the ass the power of speech, and it reasoned with him, and asked him if ever it had behaved in this manner before. And Balaam had his eyes opened, so that he saw the angel of the Lord with the drawn sword in his hand, and he bowed his head and fell flat upon his face. And the angel told him that he had displeased God, and that he would have been slain had not the ass turned back three times. Then Balaam confessed that he had sinned, and offered to turn back, but the angel said, Go with the men; but only the words that I shall speak unto thee, that thou shalt speak. So Balaam went with the princes of Balak.

When the king of Moab heard that Balaam was coming, he went out to meet him, and the prophet explained to him that he had no power to say anything save what God would put in his mouth. And Balak made a feast; and next day he took Balaam to the top of a hill where they worshipped Baal, the false god, and offered sacrifices. And Balaam went to a place apart, and God met him and gave him a reply for Balak. It was this: How shall I curse, whom God hath not cursed? or how shall I defy, whom the Lord hath not defied?

Balak was displeased at this, and twice again he tried to get Balaam to curse the people, the last time from the top of Mount Peor, where he could see the great host of Israel spread out before him. Here Balaam exclaimed, How goodly are thy tents, O Jacob, and thy tabernacles, O Israel! As the valleys are they spread forth, as gardens by the river's side, as the trees of lign-aloes which the Lord hath planted, and as cedar-trees beside the waters. He closed with the words, Blessed is he that blesseth thee, and cursed is he that curseth thee.

And Balak was more displeased than ever, but Balaam reminded him that he had told his messengers that though he were to give him a house full of silver and gold he could only utter the truth about God's chosen people. And here, with the country spread out before him, he said that the nations round about would perish, but that Israel would wax greater; and he uttered the prophecy: I shall see him, but not now; I shall behold him, but not nigh; there shall come a star out of Jacob, and a sceptre shall rise out of Israel.

Although Balak did not get Balaam to curse the children of Israel, his presence there had a bad influence over them, for he taught them to worship idols by inviting them to the feasts of the Midianites and Moabites. For this sin they were plagued by God, and many thousands of them were slain.

At the command of God Moses and Eleazar again numbered the people, to see how many men there were of twenty years and upwards fit for war. It was now found that of all the people numbered in the wilderness only two, Caleb and Joshua, were alive. These were the two spies who had brought back the truthful report from the promised land.

The time was now at hand when Moses was to die, and at God's command Joshua was appointed in his stead. Before he died Moses gathered the people together, and spoke serious and earnest words to them. He reminded them of all the goodness of the Lord in their wanderings in the wilderness, and of their frequent disobediences. He told them they were to teach the commandments of God to their children, talk about them in the house, when they were walking outside, and when they rose in the morning. And the sum of them was: Thou shalt love the Lord thy God with all thine heart, and with all thy soul, and with all thy might.

After Moses had blessed Joshua before all the people, and exhorted him to be strong and of a good courage, they went together into the tabernacle, where God spoke to them of his good pleasure regarding his chosen people. And Moses wrote all the words of the law and gave them to the Levites to keep. He also wrote a song which they were to teach to their children, and this song contained a prophecy that the time would come when all nations would rejoice with his people, when the Lord would be merciful to them again. Moses then went up from the plains of Moab to Mount Nebo, to the top of Pisgah, where God gave him a view of the promised land, which he was not to be allowed to enter. The Lord said, This is the land which I sware unto Abraham, unto Isaac, and unto Jacob, saying, I will give it unto thy seed; I have caused thee to see it with thine eyes, but thou shalt not go over thither.

And Moses was one hundred and twenty years old when he died upon the top of the mount. No man knew his burial-place, for the Lord buried him in a valley of Moab. And the people mourned for him thirty days in the plains of Moab. We read that there had not arisen in Israel a prophet like unto Moses, whom the Lord knew face to face.

And the word of the Lord came to Joshua that Moses was dead, and that he was to arise and become their leader, and take the children of Israel across the Jordan into the land of Canaan. The promise was given to him, As I was with Moses, so I will be with thee; I will not fail thee nor forsake thee. He was also commanded to be strong and of a good courage; and if he made the law of God the law of his life, then the Lord would make his way prosperous.

Joshua now began to prepare to cross the Jordan and enter the land of promise. He sent two spies across into Jericho to report as to the strength of the city; and they hid from the king of Jericho in the house of a woman named Rahab. When it was reported that they were in the city, she concealed them under some flax on the roof of the house; and when the officers came to seek for them she made them believe they had escaped. Then when the men who sought them were gone, she let the spies down over the city wall by a rope. Before doing so she made them promise that when the Israelites came and took the city, they would spare her and her friends from death. When the spies returned to the camp of Joshua, they assured him that God

THE BURIAL PLACE OF MOSES

had surely given them the land, as the people were in terror because of them.

Early in the morning Joshua led the people to the brink of the Jordan, where they stayed three days. On the morning of the fourth day, at the command of Joshua, the priests took the ark and marched forward; and as soon as their feet touched the water, the water parted before them, and they walked to the centre of the river, where they remained with the ark. The people then walked over on dry ground, as they had done through the Red Sea. And as soon as they had all passed over, the waters came back again and covered the pathway they had trodden, and flowed on as before.

As Joshua left the camp to survey the walls of Jericho, he saw a man standing with a drawn sword in his hand. And Joshua asked him whether he was for or against him, when he answered, As captain of the Lord's host am I come; and Joshua bowed down and worshipped him, for it was the Lord. And he told Joshua to cause all the men of war to march round the city once every day for six days, and the ark was also to be carried round by the priests. Seven priests were to march before the ark and blow trumpets of rams' horns. On the seventh day they were to march round Jericho seven times, and the priests were to blow with trumpets. Then when they heard a loud blast with the trumpets, the men of Israel were to shout, and the walls of Jericho would fall down, and they would be able to enter in and take possession of it. And they did as the Lord had commanded; and the last time that the priests blew with the trumpets, Joshua ordered

THE ISRAELITES PASSING THROUGH THE JORDAN

them to shout. And as they did so, the walls of the city fell flat, and they took possession of Jericho. As had been promised, Rahab, who had concealed the spies, with her father and mother and brothers, were saved, and dwelt among the children of Israel.

After Jericho was taken, Joshua sent out spies to report upon a city called Ai. And these spies reported that Ai could be easily taken by two or three thousand men. So Joshua sent up about three thousand men against the city; but the men of Ai came out after them, and drove them down the hill, smiting and killing many of them. This discouraged the Israelites, and Joshua cried to God not to deliver them up to their enemies. And the Lord commanded him to rise up from the ground, telling him that the children of Israel had sinned in keeping back some of the spoil of Jericho which the Lord had commanded them to deliver up for his service. And Joshua called out the people, and the Lord showed him the man who had sinned. His name was Achan, and he confessed that he had been tempted to take a beautiful garment and some pieces of silver and gold, and these he had hid under his tent. And they sent and found the things under Achan's tent. And Achan and his sons and daughters and all that he had were destroyed, and stones were cast upon them, and they were burned with fire. And the place where this was done was called Achor, which means "trouble." So after they had put from among them the accursed thing, God gave them the victory over the men of Ai.

While the Israelites were at Gilgal, the place at which they had rested after crossing the Jordan, the

THE FALL OF JERICHO

kings of the land banded together in order to fight against them. The people of Gibeon, knowing that the Lord was with the Israelites to give them the land, acted in a very deceitful manner. A party of the Gibeonites came to Joshua in the camp at Gilgal in order to make peace with him. Their shoes were worn out, as if they had come a long journey, their clothes were old, and the bread which they showed to Joshua was dry and mouldy-looking. Joshua and the princes of Israel, deceived by these signs, thought that these Gibeonites had really come a long journey, and without laying the matter before the Lord made a treaty of peace with them. When it was discovered that they had only come a little way to the camp, and that they were one of the tribes which God had called upon them to destroy, Joshua summoned them before him, and asked them why they had acted thus. The Gibeonites answered that it was because they were sore afraid of their lives that they had done this thing. But because Joshua had promised in a solemn manner not to kill them, he delivered them out of the hands of the people, but ordered that they should be made hewers of wood and drawers of water for the Israelites and for the altar of the Lord.

When the king of Jerusalem heard what these Gibeonites had done in making peace with the Israelites, he was afraid, and united with other four kings, and came up against Gibeon. Then the Gibeonites asked Joshua to come with his army and help them against these five kings. And the Lord told Joshua not to be afraid, for he had delivered these enemies into his hand. So Joshua with his fighting men went up to the help of the Gibeonites, and the five kings fled before them. And as they were fleeing the Lord rained great hailstones from heaven upon them, so that more perished by the hailstones than were slain by the sword.

And as the Israelites pursued their enemies, the daylight began to fail, and Joshua prayed to God to lengthen the day. And God did so by causing the sun to stand still upon Gibeon and the moon in the valley of Ajalon, so that the people had light until the armies of the five kings were destroyed. But the five kings themselves escaped, and were hidden in a cave, to which Joshua caused the people to roll great stones. So they were prisoners there, and were taken out and hanged when the battle was finished. And the Lord was with the Israelites, and delivered into their hand one city after another, until they took the whole land, when they had rest for a time from war.

Joshua being now old, and having not long to live, he gathered the people together before the tabernacle, and cast lots for them before the Lord, in order that the land might be equally divided among the tribes. To the Levites no inheritance in land was given; but they received forty-eight cities, of which six were to be cities of refuge, to which those who had shed blood unwittingly might fly and be safe. And thus the Lord gave unto Israel all the land which he swore to give unto their fathers; and they possessed it, and dwelt therein. And the Lord gave them rest round about. And the Reubenites and the Gadites, and the half tribe Manasseh, who had been foremost in fighting against their enemies, returned laden with spoil to the land on the other side of Jordan which had been given to them by Moses. And they built an altar on a high hill on the borders of their land, to show that they were one in faith with the people of Israel.

Before Joshua died he bade farewell to the elders and chiefs, and told them to take good heed unto themselves that they loved the Lord their God. He also gathered all the people to him at Shechem, and reviewed their wonderful history, and asked them to choose that day whom they would serve, adding, As for me and my house, we will serve the Lord. And the people answered that they also would serve the Lord. And Joshua made a covenant with them, and wrote it in the book of the law of God. He also set up a stone pillar as a witness, under an oak-tree at Shechem. And so Joshua let the people depart every man unto his inheritance. And Joshua was one hundred and ten years old when he died, and they buried him in Mount Ephraim.

CHAPTER VII

THE TIME OF THE JUDGES—DEBORAH AND BARAK DEFEAT THE CANAANITES—THE PEOPLE OPPRESSED BY MIDIANITES—GIDEON DELIVERS THEM—THE STORY OF JEPHTHAH.

WE come now to the period in the history of the children of Israel called the time of the JUDGES. God had allowed many of the enemies of Israel still to live in Canaan in order that he might prove his people and see if they would drive them out and destroy them. The tribes of Judah and Simeon were the first to go to war against the Canaanites and Perizzites, and the other tribes followed; but they displeased God in that, although they conquered the heathen, they did not utterly drive them out and destroy them, as they had been commanded. So these heathen people became as thorns in their sides, and their gods became snares to the Israelites; for very soon they began to marry with them, and to commit idolatry. And God punished them by allowing them to fall into the hand of the king of Mesopotamia, whom they served eight years. At the end of that time the Lord gave his Spirit to Othniel, who was the first of the Judges; and the Israelites went out against the king of Mesopotamia, and freed themselves from his yoke.

Othniel judged the people for forty years, and after his death they again fell into idolatry. Another punishment came upon them, for they fell into the hands of Eglon, king of Moab, who, with Ammon and Amalek to help him, conquered them. After eighteen years had passed, and when the people had repented, another judge called Ehud was sent to them. And Ehud killed the king of Moab as he sat in his summer parlor. Then he summoned the people together, and led them against the army of Moab, and defeated it with great slaughter.

The next judge over the people was Shamgar, who with an ox-goad slew six hundred of the Philistines. After that, a prophetess named Deborah was chosen to be judge over the people, who at that time were servants of the king of Canaan. And Deborah chose a man named Barak, and told him to lead ten thousand men of Israel against the king of Canaan, and the Lord would give him the victory. But Barak would only go if Deborah went with him; and she consented, but told him that the captain of the Canaanites would fall into the hands of a woman.

Sisera, the Canaanitish captain, met the men of Israel with his nine hundred chariots of iron, and there was a great battle, in which the Israelites prevailed. A heavy storm flooded the river Kishon, where the battle was fought, so that it overflowed its banks, and swept away many of the combatants. Sisera escaped to the tent of Heber the Kenite, who was absent, but Jael his wife welcomed Sisera, and concealed him in her tent beneath a mantle. Being faint and weary from the battle she gave him milk, and he fell asleep. After this he awoke, and asked Jael to stand in the tent-door, so that if any one came after him, she might answer he was not there. She did so, pretending to be friendly with him.

Sisera, feeling secure, again fell asleep, and while he was sleeping Jael took a hammer and a nail, and drove it through his temples. And thus Sisera died by the hand of a woman. And as Barak passed that way Jael asked him in and showed him Sisera lying dead on the ground. And Deborah and Barak made a song about this victory, which ends thus: So let all thine enemies perish, O Lord: but let them that love him be as the sun when he goeth forth in his might.

After this the land had rest for forty years, when the Israelites again did evil, and were punished by being allowed to fall into the hands of the Midianites. They oppressed the people grievously, so that they were glad to take refuge in the dens and caves of the mountains. The Amalekites joined with the Midianites, and they overran the country, and destroyed the corn, the vineyards, and the olive-yards. In their distress the people cried to God, when a prophet was sent to reprove them for their sin. A judge was also raised up named Gideon, of the tribe of Manasseh. The call of the Lord came to Gideon when he was thrashing wheat. The angel of God said to him, The Lord is with thee, thou mighty man of valor. And Gideon said, O my Lord, if the Lord be with us, why then is all this befallen us? Then the Lord promised to be with him, and told him that if he led the Israelites up against the Midianites, he would smite them as one man. Gideon could scarcely believe that all this was true, and asked for a sign. He then went and brought a kid and some unleavened cakes, which he put under the oak-tree for the angel to eat. The angel asked him to lay them upon a rock near by; which Gideon having done, the angel touched them with the end of a staff, and immediately fire came out of the rock and burnt the offering; and the angel departed. Then Gideon overthrew the altar which his father Joash had erected to Baal, and built one to the God of Israel.

When the Midianites came and encamped in Jezreel, the Spirit of the Lord came upon Gideon, and he sounded a trumpet, and called the children of Israel together to fight against them. Before going he sought for a sign that the Lord was with him. And he laid a fleece of wool on the floor, and asked that if God meant to save Israel by his hand, dew would be sent upon the fleece, but none upon the ground. So Gideon waited all night for an answer to his prayer. In the morning the fleece was wet, but the ground was dry. But he asked for yet another sign, that this time the ground should be wet and his fleece dry. And it was so; for it was dry upon the fleece only, and there was dew upon all the ground.

Gideon, being now assured that the Lord was with him, gathered the Israelites together to do battle against Midian. But God commanded him that he should take but few with him, that the glory should be his only. So Gideon told all those who were fearful and afraid to depart from him at Mount Gilead. This caused twenty-two thousand men to leave him, and he was left with ten thousand. But the Lord said these were yet too many, and commanded that a test was to be made to be applied to decide who were to go with him. The army was taken to the brink of the river, and those only who dipped their hands into the water and lapped it like a dog were chosen. Those who had knelt to drink were rejected, so that Gideon had now only three hundred men wherewith to go against the Midianites.

Then God commanded Gideon to go down to the camp of the Midianites and take with him his servant, and he would hear something which would help him to be strong and of a good courage. So Gideon and his servant went during the night and visited the camp of Midian; and they found the host to be like grasshoppers for multitude, and their camels without number. As they drew near to the camp Gideon heard one man telling his fellow a strange dream which he had had. His dream was that "a cake of barley-bread tumbled into the host of Midian, and came unto a tent, and smote it that it fell and overturned it." And the other man answered that doubtless his dream meant that Gideon the Israelite was to come up against them, and gain the victory over them.

When Gideon heard this dream he worshipped God, and returned to his army, and said to them, Arise, for the Lord hath delivered into your hand the host of Midian. Then he divided his three hundred men into companies of a hundred each, and to every man he gave a trumpet, and a pitcher with a lighted lamp within it. Then he sent one of these divisions to one part of the valley, and one to another, while he led the third himself. And so they marched quietly on in the darkness towards the enemy. And Gideon said, When I blow with a trumpet, I and all that are with me, then blow ye the trumpets also on every side of all the camp, and say, The sword of the Lord and of Gideon. And when they did so, the Midianites were startled by the noise of the trumpets and the breaking of the earthen pitchers, and when they saw the burning lamps it caused great confusion amongst them, and they fought against one another in the darkness. And the Lord made them afraid of the men of Israel, so that they fled towards the river Jordan. And the Israelites pursued after them, joined by numbers of their brethren, and followed them to Mount Ephraim. And Gideon slew two of their kings, the very same who had slain his own brothers long before. And he came to Jordan with his followers, and passed over, "faint, yet pursuing." So the land had rest forty years.

After Gideon's death the Israelites again forgot the God of their fathers, and fell into sin. Then one of Gideon's seventy sons, named Abimelech, wishing to be made king over Israel, went to Shechem, his mother's city, and hired men, who went with him to his father's house, and he slew all his brothers but one, named Jotham, who escaped. He then returned to Shechem, and his mother's brethren made him king.

But Abimelech was at last punished for his wickedness. Having come up against a city called Thebez, where there was a strong tower, in which the people of the city had taken refuge, he would have burned it, but a woman dropped a piece of a millstone upon his head, which broke his skull. Then he called upon his armor-bearer to draw his sword and slay him, so that men might not say that

THE SWORD OF THE LORD AND OF GIDEON.

a woman slew him. And so he died. And at his death the men he had gathered together returned every man to his place.

After the death of Abimelech the Israelites were ruled by several judges, and on the death of one of them called Jair, they again became idolaters. And the Lord was displeased with them, and allowed them to fall into the hands of the Philistines. In their distress they cried unto God and confessed their sin; but he answered them at first in words of reproof, asking them if he had not delivered them from the Egyptians and from the enemies they had encountered in Canaan, and telling them to go and cry unto the gods they had chosen. And they confessed their sin, and the Lord was grieved for the misery of his people.

Then the Ammonites gathered together and encamped in Gilead, and the children of Israel encamped in Mizpeh. And the princes and people of Gilead longed for a leader who would take them up against the Ammonites. And they bethought them of a valiant man named Jephthah, whom they had formerly ill-treated, and who had fled from them. And they asked him to come and lead them against the Ammonites. But Jephthah upbraided them for having expelled him before, and asked them whether, if he defeated Ammon, they would make him their head. And the elders took God to witness that they would do according to Jephthah's word. So he went to the camp of Israel, and took the command, and sent a message to the king of Ammon asking why he made war against them. And the king, who only wanted an excuse for going to war, said it was because the Israelites had taken his lands when they had come up out of Egypt. Jephthah sent back word that it was not so. And the Spirit of the Lord came upon him, and he went forth to meet the king of Ammon; but before going he made a solemn vow to God that if he gained the victory, whatsoever came forth from his house to meet him on his return should surely be the Lord's, and he would offer it up as a burnt-offering.

The army of Israel was successful, and twenty cities were taken. And when Jephthah returned to his house, his daughter came out to meet him with her maidens playing on timbrels. And she was his only child. Jephthah, when he saw her, remembered his promise to the Lord, and he rent his clothes, and said, Alas, my daughter! and told her of his vow. And she said unto her father, If thou hast opened thy mouth unto the Lord, do to me according to that which hath proceeded out of thy mouth. She only asked that she might be allowed to wander for two months among the mountains lamenting her fate, along with her companions. She went, and at the end of two months Jephthah fulfilled his vow. Ever afterwards it was a custom in Israel for the young women to spend four days among the hills of Gilead lamenting Jephthah's daughter.

CHAPTER VIII

THE BIRTH OF SAMSON—HE IS CALLED TO BE JUDGE—HIS DEATH—THE STORY OF RUTH—THE BIRTH OF SAMUEL—ELI AND HIS SONS—SAMUEL CHOSEN TO BE PROPHET AND JUDGE.

WHILE the children of Israel were again servants to the Philistines, there lived in Zorah a man named Manoah, of the family of the Danites, and his wife had no children. And the angel of the Lord appeared to the woman and told her she would have a son, who was to be a Nazarite from his birth (that is to say, he was to be set apart for the Lord's service, and drink no wine, and allow his hair to grow long), and was to help to free the people from the tyranny of the Philistines.

The angel also appeared to Manoah, and revealed the same thing to him. And he offered a kid upon a rock as a burnt-offering; and when the flame went up from the altar the angel ascended in the flame. And Manoah was afraid, and said, We have seen God. When the son was born to Manoah and his wife, they named him Samson; and he grew and was blessed of the Lord. When he was of age he went to Timnath, and saw there a Philistine woman whom he wished to make his wife. And he told his father and mother, who were displeased at his choice. But they went down to Timnath with him to see the woman, and on their way a young lion roared at Samson, and the Lord gave him strength to slay the lion as easily as if it had been a kid, without any weapon save his hands. On going down after a time to Timnath to take the woman to wife, he turned aside to look at the carcass of the lion, when he saw that a swarm of bees had made honey there. So he took a piece of the honeycomb in his hands, and walked down eating it. He also gave some to his father and mother, but did not tell them where he had got it. At the marriage-feast at Timnath he gave his guests a riddle, and said that whoever answered it before the seven days of the feast were ended was to receive thirty suits of clothing; and if they could not answer it, then they were to give him thirty suits of clothing. The riddle was: Out of the eater came forth meat, and out of the strong came forth sweetness. The Philistines could not expound the riddle, and on the seventh day they came to Samson's wife and threatened to burn her and all her relations unless she got the explanation from her husband, and declared it to them. Samson, in answer to her inquiry, did not tell her at first; but when she wept and entreated him he did so. And she at once told it to the Philistines. So on the last day of the feast they pretended they had discovered the riddle; but Samson knew his wife must have told them. In order to get the thirty suits of clothing for the Philistines, Samson went down to Ashkelon, and slew thirty men there, and brought away their garments.

At the time of wheat-harvest Samson went again to Timnath to visit his wife, and took a kid with him. But he was told that she was his wife no longer, and that she had been given to another man. So

Samson was angry, and catching three hundred foxes, he tied blazing pieces of wood to their tails, and let them loose among the corn of the Philistines. And the corn was all burned up, as well as the grape-vines and the olive-trees. When the Philistines discovered that Samson had done this, they took his wife and her father, and burned them with fire. Samson told them he would be avenged of them, and he slew them with a great slaughter. And afterwards he went to live on a rock called Etam.

Then the Philistines came to Etam to take him, and alarmed the Israelites, who asked Samson why he had slain the Philistines. And Samson replied, As they did unto me so have I done unto them. And the Israelites took him and bound him with two new cords, and gave him up to the Philistines; but when he was brought to their camp he snapped the cords as if they had been thread. And finding the jawbone of an ass, he took it and slew a thousand men of the Philistines with it. After he had thrown the bone away he felt thirsty, and the Lord clave a hollow place in the jawbone, and there came out water; so he drank and was refreshed.

After this Samson went to a city of the Philistines called Gaza, and entered the house of a woman named Delilah. When the people knew that he was in their city they shut the gates, and said they would kill him in the morning. But Samson rose up at midnight, and finding the gates shut, he pulled up the two gate-posts, and bore the gates to a hill near the city. Then the Philistines went to Delilah, and asked her to find out wherein Samson's

SAMSON SLAYING THE PHILISTINES

great strength lay, that they might take him and do as they pleased with him. Samson told Delilah that if he were to be bound with seven green twigs he would not be able to break through them. So he allowed her to bind him with seven green twigs, and she said, The Philistines be upon thee, Samson. But he broke these twigs as a thread of tow is broken when it toucheth the fire. Twice more he mocked her, first by telling her to bind him with new ropes, and then to plait his hair; both of which being tried failed as before. At last he told her the truth, that he was a Nazarite from his birth, that his hair had never been cut, and that if it was shaven from his head he would be weak as other men. As Delilah was a wicked woman she took advantage of his confidence, and had his hair shaven while he was asleep, and he was taken captive by the Philistines, who put out his eyes, bound him with fetters, and made him grind in prison. While in prison his hair began to grow again, and doubtless, repenting of his sin, his wonderful strength began to return.

One day the lords of the Philistines made a great feast to their idol Dagon, and being glad that Samson was now in their hands they sent for him that he might make sport for them. When he came, they set him between two pillars of the idol temple; and both the roof and the inside of the house were full of people, all the lords of the Philistines being there. And Samson asked the boy who led him to allow him to feel the pillars upon which the house stood. Then he prayed the Lord to give him strength but this once, that he might be avenged of

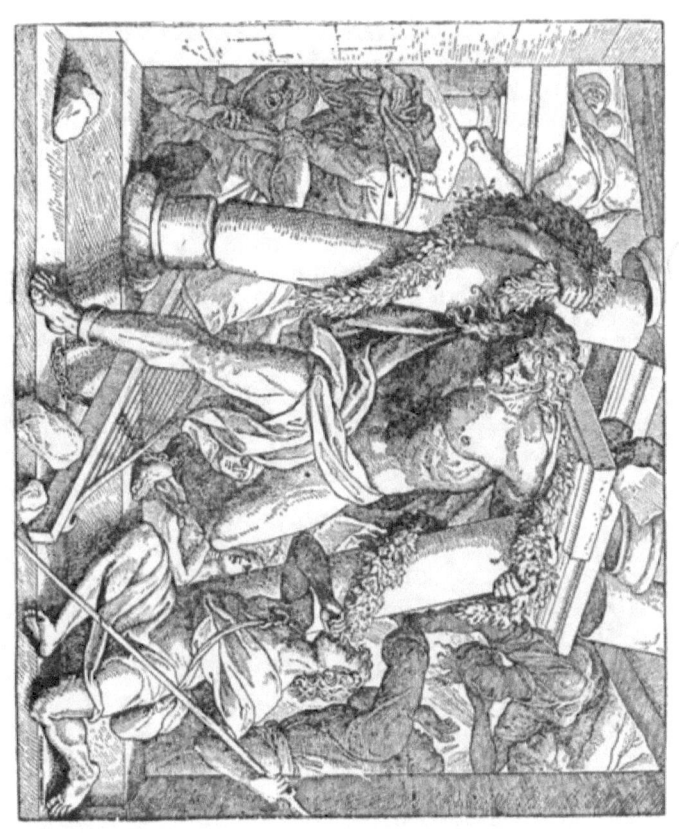

SAMSON DESTROYING THE TEMPLE

the Philistines. And putting forth his hands he took hold of the two middle pillars upon which the house rested, and bowing himself, the house fell and killed all the people that were on the roof and within it. And so Samson died, after being judge in Israel for twenty years.

At the time when the judges ruled in Israel there lived a man in Beth-lehem-judah named Elimelech, with his wife Naomi, and his two sons, Mahlon and Chilion. There was a famine in the land, and they journeyed to Moab to get food. There Elimelech died; and after a time his two sons, Mahlon and Chilion, who had married Orpah and Ruth, women of Moab, also died. When Naomi heard that there was again food to be had in her own country, she started to return from Moab, and her daughters-in-law began the journey with her. But she was not willing that they should leave their own country; so she advised them to return. She kissed them, and they wept and said they would not leave her. Naomi again told them they would be happier in their own land, and that they ought not to leave it. Orpah at last returned home; but Ruth, although urged by her, clave unto her, and said, Entreat me not to leave thee, or to return from following after thee: for whither thou goest, I will go; and where thou lodgest, I will lodge: thy people shall be my people, and thy God my God: where thou diest, will I die, and there will I be buried: the Lord do so to me, and more also, if aught but death part thee and me. Naomi seeing that Ruth was steadfast left off speaking to her, and they journeyed together.

And they came to Beth-lehem at the time of barley-harvest; and as they were poor, Ruth went to the fields to glean after the reapers, and it so happened that the field to which she went belonged to Boaz, a kinsman of Elimelech's. Boaz came out into the field, and seeing a stranger gleaning, he asked who she was. The reapers told him that this was Ruth, the daughter-in-law of Naomi, who had come with her from Moab. Then Boaz spoke kindly to her, and told her to remain in that field and glean, and also invited her to share the refreshments along with the reapers. Ruth bowed low in acknowledgment, and thanked him for his kindness. Boaz told her that he had heard of all she had done to her mother-in-law, and said, The Lord recompense thy work, and a full reward be given thee of the Lord God of Israel, under whose wings thou art come to trust. The kindness of Boaz did not end here. He told his young men to allow her to glean even among the sheaves, where the corn was thickest on the ground, and also to let fall some handfuls on purpose for her. In the evening Ruth carried home to Naomi what she had been gleaning, and told her in whose field she had been gathering the corn, and how well she had been treated. When Naomi heard this, she told Ruth that Boaz was a friend of Elimelech's, her father-in-law. So Ruth gleaned in the fields of Boaz all the time of barley-harvest and wheat-harvest; and when the reaping and thrashing were over Naomi bade her go and tell Boaz that she was a relative of his, for according to Jewish custom, being her nearest of kin, he ought to care for her. Boaz received her kindly and sent her back to Naomi with the promise that it would be well with her.

That day Boaz went to the city-gate and waited, and he stopped a near kinsman of Elimelech's, and then asked ten chief men of the city to come and listen to what he had to say. Boaz told this kinsman how Naomi had returned from Moab, and wished to sell some land that belonged to her late husband, and as he was a kinsman he should have the first chance of buying it. The man was willing to buy the land, but when he heard that he must also marry Ruth he refused. So Boaz said he was willing to purchase the land and marry Ruth; and he asked the ten elders to witness the bargain. And thus the dutiful and affectionate Ruth was richly provided for. Boaz and Ruth lived at Beth-lehem, and they had a son born to them called Obed; and the son of Obed was Jesse, and Jesse was the father of David, the sweet singer and the second king of Israel.

While Samson was judge in Israel there lived in Mount Ephraim a man called Elkanah, and his wife Hannah had no children. And she came to the tabernacle to pray; and Eli, the high priest, seeing her lips moving but uttering no sound, thought she was overcome with strong drink. But Hannah answered, No, my lord, I am a woman of a sorrowful spirit, and have poured out my heart before the Lord. Then Eli bade her go in peace, and said, The God of Israel grant thee the petition thou hast asked of him. The request that Hannah had made in prayer was that she might have a son; and she vowed if God should grant her request that her son would be dedicated to the service of the Lord.

And a son was born to Hannah in answer to her prayer, and she called his name Samuel, which means, "Asked of the Lord." When the child was still young she took him, with an offering for a sacrifice, to Shiloh, where the tabernacle was, to render thanks to God, who had heard her prayer. And she told Eli why she had come, and left her child there with him to serve in the tabernacle. And the child Samuel was dressed in the linen garment worn by those who served there, and God was with him.

And one day there came a man of God to Eli, the high priest, to reprove him because of the wickedness of his sons, and because he had not punished them for their evil ways. And it was told him that the judgment of God would come upon them, for they would both die in one day, and not one of his family would succeed him in the priesthood. A faithful priest was to be raised up to succeed him, who would walk before the Lord forever.

One night while the child Samuel waited upon Eli, a voice called him, and thinking it was that of the high priest, he answered, Here am I, and ran to him, saying, Here am I ; for thou calledst me. Eli told him to go and lie down, as he did not call him. Twice again Samuel heard the voice, and went to Eli, when the high priest at last saw that it was the Lord who had been calling Samuel. He therefore told him to go and lie down ; and if he heard the voice again he was to answer, Speak, Lord ; for thy servant heareth. So Samuel went and lay down in his place. And the Lord came and stood, and called as at other times, Samuel, Samuel. Then Samuel answered, Speak ; for thy servant heareth. And God spake to Samuel, and told him of the great punishment he was about to bring upon Eli's sons. Samuel lay until the morning; and when Eli asked him what the message of the Lord had been, Samuel unwillingly told him all the truth. And Eli, with resignation said, It is the Lord; let him do what seemeth him good. After this Samuel grew, and the Lord was with him, and it became known that he had been chosen to be a prophet of the Lord.

About this time the Israelites went out against the Philistines to battle, and they were smitten, and about four thousand of them were slain. The elders of Israel wondered when the army came back to the camp why the Lord had not given them the victory, and they brought out the ark of the covenant from Shiloh, that it might save them from their enemies. And the ark was taken, and Eli's two sons, Hophni and Phinehas, who were with it, were amongst the slain. Then a messenger ran from the camp to Shiloh, and found Eli sitting by the wayside to hear news of the battle. When the messenger told him of the death of his sons, and that the ark of God was in the hands of the enemy, Eli fell backward from the seat where he was sitting, and his neck was broken, so that he died. Eli had judged Israel forty years, and was ninety-eight years old when he died.

Then the Philistines carried away the ark to Ashdod, a city on the sea-coast, where they placed it in the temple of their idol Dagon. Now Dagon had the body of a man and the tail of a fish, and next morning when they came in they found that the idol had fallen upon its face before the ark. They set up their idol again, but next morning they again found it lying on its face, and only the stump left standing. A painful disease next broke out amongst the people of the city, and they knew it was because of the ark being in their midst. So they removed it to Gath; but the same thing happened there. Next they took it to Ekron, when the Ekronites begged the lords of the Philistines to take it back to Shiloh. So they took the advice of their priests and magicians, and it was sent to the city of the Levites.

CHAPTER IX

SAUL CHOSEN TO BE KING—HE DEFEATS THE ENE-MIES OF THE PEOPLE—SAMUEL DISPLACES HIM FOR DISOBEDIENCE—DAVID ANOINTED KING—HE SLAYS A PHILISTINE GIANT—AND MARRIES SAUL'S DAUGHTER—SAUL'S ANGER AT DAVID.

AFTER twenty years had passed, the Israelites began to lament after the Lord; and Samuel told them if they wished with all their hearts to return to the Lord, they must put away their idols from amongst them, and prepare to serve the Lord only. So Samuel gathered them together at Mizpeh, where they fasted and confessed their sins. When the Philistines heard that the people were at Mizpeh, they came up against them, and Samuel entreated the Lord on their behalf, and a thunderstorm was sent which discomfited the Philistines. And Samuel set up a stone there, which he called Ebenezer, meaning, "Hitherto hath the Lord helped us."

When Samuel grew old he made his sons judges over Israel, but they were dishonest and unfaithful. And the people came to Samuel and asked that they might have a king to rule over them, like the other nations. Samuel was displeased, and laid the matter before the Lord, and he commanded Samuel, notwithstanding the ingratitude of the people, to grant their request, but also to warn them that their condition would not be the same under a king as it had been before; for a king would oppress them, tax them, and take their sons and daughters to be his servants.

Now there was a mighty man of the tribe of Benjamin, named Kish, who had a son called Saul, and there was not among all the people a goodlier person than he. One day Saul went out in search of his father's asses, which had strayed, and he came to Samuel, the prophet and judge, to see if he could tell him where they were. And the Lord had warned Samuel that the man who was to be king over Israel would come that day. So when Samuel met him he bade him stay with him until the morrow. And on the morrow he anointed Saul with oil, and told him that God had chosen him to be captain over his inheritance, and that on his way home he would witness various signs which would confirm the truth of what he had said. So the Spirit of the Lord came upon Saul, and he joined a company of the prophets, and prophesied with them.

And it became a proverb amongst them, Is Saul also among the prophets?

After that Samuel again called the people together at Mizpeh, and Saul and his friends were there. And Samuel told the people his message from the Lord, that they had rejected him who had brought them out of the land of Egypt, in asking that a king should rule over them. Then he caused each tribe to pass before him, until the tribe of Benjamin was chosen, and from among the families of Benjamin the family to which Saul belonged was chosen. And Saul was called, for he had hidden himself; but God showed them that he was amongst the baggage of the encampment. And when they found him, he stood higher than any of the people from his shoulders and upward. Then Samuel asked the people to look upon the man whom the Lord had chosen to be their king. And the people shouted, God save the king. Then Samuel made known to the people the way in which they were to be governed, and wrote it in a book, which was laid up before the Lord. And the people departed to their own homes.

On returning to Gibeah, where he lived, news was brought to Saul one day that the Ammonites had come up against Jabesh-Gilead, and would only spare the city on condition that the people in it would consent to have their right eyes put out. And Saul cut a yoke of oxen in pieces, and sent portions to the different tribes, saying, that if they did not follow him, then their oxen would be cut in pieces in like manner. And many thousands of the people went up with Saul against the Ammonites, and they scattered them, so that two of them were not left together. And the hearts of the people began to trust in the king whom the Lord had chosen for them.

Then Samuel called a great assembly of the people at Gilgal to renew the kingdom before the Lord. And Samuel spoke to the people, telling them he was now old and gray-headed, and appealing to them whether he had not walked before them honestly until that day, having neither defrauded them nor oppressed them. And the people said it was so. Then Samuel rehearsed to them all the way the Lord had led them since they came up out of Egypt, and how they had often rebelled against him, and he had forgiven them. He exhorted them to fear the Lord, and serve him with truth, for if they should continue to do wickedly, he would consume both them and their king.

Saul was not long king before he attacked the Philistines in Geba. And the Philistines gathered themselves together to fight with Israel, and they had thirty thousand chariots, and six thousand horsemen, and a great multitude of fighting men. And the men of Israel had to hide themselves in holes of the rocks, and among the trees, and in pits. Then Saul went to Gilgal to see Samuel and ask his advice; and the king was to wait for the prophet seven days. But when the seven days passed, and the prophet came not to tell him what to do, Saul offered a burnt-offering himself. Then Samuel appeared, and told him that because of his disobedience none of his family would inherit the throne, but that God would choose in place of them a man after his own heart.

Jonathan, the son of Saul, at this time did a very brave thing: he went out with no one but the young man who carried his armor, and trusting that God would help him, he killed twenty men. This caused a panic in the camp of the Philistines, and Saul hearing of it, followed it up, and gained a great victory over them.

After this time Samuel told Saul that the Lord wished him to go against the Amalekites, the people that had troubled Israel in the wilderness, and utterly to destroy them. And Saul smote the Amalekites with great slaughter, and came and told Samuel that he had carried out the command of the Lord, and destroyed the Amalekites. Samuel asked what meant then the bleating of sheep and the lowing of oxen that he heard. Saul said he had spared them for a sacrifice to the Lord. Samuel told him that to obey was better than sacrifice. The Lord had ordered him to consume the Amalekites and all that they possessed, and he had not done so; and for this disobedience he would be cast aside, and would be no longer king.

And God commanded Samuel to go to Jesse, the grandson of Boaz and Ruth, and take anointing oil with him, for he had provided a king for Israel among Jesse's sons. And Samuel went to Beth-lehem, where he made a solemn sacrifice to the Lord before the people. And when Samuel saw Eliab, Jesse's eldest son, he thought he was the man who should be chosen, for he was beautiful to look upon. But God told him that Eliab was not the man; he did not judge by the outward appearance, but looked upon the heart. And all the seven sons of Jesse were passed before him, but Samuel told Jesse that God had chosen none of these. Then Samuel asked Jesse whether he had any other sons. Jesse replied that there was yet the youngest, who was keeping sheep. And Samuel said, Send and fetch him. When David, the shepherd boy, came, he looked ruddy and beautiful, and the Lord commanded Samuel to anoint him, as he was to be the new king in Israel. So Samuel anointed David, and the Spirit of the Lord was with him from that day forward.

At that time the Spirit of the Lord left Saul, and an evil spirit troubled him. In order to drive away this melancholy spirit, his servants proposed that a skilful musician should be sent for to play upon the harp before him. And when Saul agreed, they said that there was a son of Jesse the Beth-lehemite, who was a skilful player upon the harp, and a valiant man, and comely, and that the Lord was with him. So Saul sent for David, and he found favor in the eyes of Saul; and when the evil spirit came upon him, then David took his harp and played upon it, and the evil spirit departed.

After this the Philistines gathered together for battle, and Saul went against them, and the three eldest sons of Jesse followed him, but David returned to keep his father's sheep. And one day his father sent him to the camp with provisions for his brothers. So he left his sheep in charge of another keeper, and reached the camp just as the Israelites were ready to go forth against the Philistines. When he was talking with his brethren, a giant called Goliath came out from the ranks of the Philistines, and challenged any one of the Israelites to come forth and do battle with him. If an Israelite should kill him, then the battle would be gained by the Israelites; but if, on the other hand, he should kill the Israelite, then they must serve the Philistines. Now all the Israelites were afraid of this giant, he was so tall and fierce-looking. He had a helmet of brass on his head, was covered with armor, and carried a great spear in his hand, and before him went a man who held up a shield for his defence.

David heard the haughty words of the Philistine giant, and asked further about him, and found that whoever should kill him would receive a great reward and one of the king's daughters in marriage. Eliab, David's brother, reproved him for his pride and naughtiness in asking questions about the Philistine. But David's words were told to Saul, who sent for him, and said to him that being but a youth he was not able to go against such a mighty man of war. Then David said to the king, Thy servant kept his father's sheep, and there came a lion, and a bear, and took a lamb out of the flock, and I went out after him, and smote him, and delivered it out of his mouth; and when he arose against me, I caught him by his beard, and smote him, and slew him. Thy servant slew both the lion and the bear; and this uncircumcised Philistine shall be as one of them, seeing he hath defied the armies of the living God. And Saul said, Go, and the Lord be with thee. Then Saul armed David with his armor, and David girded himself with the king's sword; but because he had not proved them he put down the king's sword and put off the armor again, and instead, took his staff in his hand, and chose him five smooth stones out of the brook, and put them in a shepherd's bag which he had, even in a scrip; and his sling was in his hand; and he drew near to the Philistine. And the Philistine came on, and drew near unto David; and the man that bare the shield went before him. And when the Philistine looked about, and saw David, he disdained him, and doubted not but that he would slay the young man who had rashly ventured to come out against him. But the Lord was with David; and he took a stone from his bag, and placed it in his sling, and aiming it at the giant it pierced his forehead, and he fell forward on his face upon the earth. Then David ran up and cut off Goliath's head with his sword in sight of both the armies. And he was welcomed with a shout of triumph from the camp of Israel, and they pursued the terror-stricken Philistines to the city of Ekron. When David returned, bearing Goliath's head, Saul asked whose son he was; and David replied that he was the son of Jesse, the Beth-lehemite. From that time David went no more home to his father's house.

David speedily formed a close friendship with Jonathan, the son of Saul. The soul of Jonathan was knit with the soul of David, and Jonathan loved him as his own soul. In token of his friendship Jonathan gave to David his own armor, even to his sword, and to his bow and his girdle. But King Saul was jealous of David when he heard the people singing, Saul hath slain his thousands, and David his tens of thousands. And when David played before Saul next day, an evil spirit came upon him,

DAVID SLAYS GOLIATH

and he threw a javelin, or spear, at him to kill him. But David stepped aside, and it missed him. Then Saul threw it once more, but David again stepped aside.

After that Saul sent out David from before him, and he became captain of a band of soldiers. He was twice sent to fight with the Philistines, because Saul hoped he might be slain. The king had begun to hate David, and purposed in his heart to kill him; but Jonathan warned him of his father's intention. After this, war broke out again, and David gained another victory over the Philistines, which made Saul hate him the more; and when David was playing before him, he again threw his javelin at him that he might kill him. But David stepped aside, and fled. He went to his own house, whither Saul sent messengers to take him, but Michal his wife let him down through a window, so that they could not see him. Then she put an image in the bed, with a pillow beneath it, so that it might seem that David was there; which gave him time to fly from his pursuers. And Saul was very angry with his daughter Michal when he found she had deceived him.

David fled to Ramah, and told Samuel all that Saul had done; and afterwards at Naioth he met with Jonathan, and told him also. Now Saul was to have a feast on the next day, and it was agreed between Jonathan and David that David should be absent, and Jonathan should try to find out whether Saul really meant to kill David. On the second day of the feast Saul asked Jonathan why David was not there. And Jonathan made answer that he

DAVID AND JONATHAN

had asked permission to go to Beth-lehem to offer sacrifice there with his family. And Saul was angry with Jonathan because of his friendship with David, and threw a javelin at him. From this Jonathan was certain that Saul had determined to slay David; so he went out to a place where he had arranged to meet him, and told him that his father meant to kill him. And Jonathan warned David to flee and hide himself from his father. And they made a vow of perpetual friendship.

David went first to the city of Nob, where the tabernacle was; and next to the Philistine city of Gath, where he was recognized, and where he feigned himself mad. Next he took refuge in the cave of Adullam, where many who were in debt or discontented joined him. After this a prophet told his brethren and friends and David to go to the land of Judah. And Saul was at Gibeah, and he was told how David, when at Nob, had been helped by Ahimelech the priest, who had given him the shewbread from the tabernacle to eat, and also the sword of Goliath the Philistine. This made Saul angry, and he sent and slew many of the priests by the hand of a wicked man called Doeg, an Edomite. But Abiathar, one of the priests, escaped and told David.

Then David heard that the Philistines had come up against a city of Judah called Keilah, and he asked the Lord if he might go up and punish them. And the Lord said unto David, Go. And David went with his small band of men and took the city. When Saul heard that David was at Keilah, he tried to entrap him, but David fled to a wood, where

Jonathan visited him and comforted him. David now fled from Saul into the wilderness of En-gedi, and Saul's army followed him to take him. And David and his men hid in a cave, and Saul without knowing they were there went into it. And David's men wished their master to kill him; but David only went up softly behind him, and secretly cut off a piece of his robe and took it away. When Saul left the cave David followed him, and saluted him, and asked him why he should think that he meant to do him harm; seeing that when he had had an opportunity of killing him in the cave he had not lifted up his hand against him. This appeal melted the heart of Saul, and he said, Is this thy voice, my son David? and he wept, saying that David was more righteous than he, for he had returned good for evil. And he asked David to swear that he would not cut off his seed after him, adding, The Lord reward thee for the good that thou hast done unto me this day. And David sware unto Saul.

While David was in the wilderness of Paran he sent for some food for his men to a rich man named Nabal. Now although David and his men had guarded Nabal's flocks in the wilderness, he was ungrateful, and would give them nothing. And in the anger of his heart David commanded his men to go and punish him. But Nabal's wife, Abigail, heard what David had purposed, and unknown to her husband, she prepared a present of loaves of bread, and wine, and sheep, and raisins, and figs and parched corn, and presented it to David and his men as they were coming to wreak their vengeance on her husband. So David's wrath was appeased, and when Nabal died shortly after, Abigail became David's wife.

Then the Ziphites, who had before been unfriendly to David, went and told Saul where to find him; so the king, whose heart had again turned against David, came out with his men into the wilderness after him. David, warned by his spies, found out where Saul had encamped, and taking his nephew Abishai, they went boldly down one night into Saul's tent, passed the sleeping soldiers, and bore away the spear of the king and the bottle of water from beside his pillow. Then going to a hill near at hand, they shouted to Saul's men, and upbraiding them, showed them the king's spear and the cruse of water they had taken. And Saul knew David's voice, and when David asked him why he hunted him thus, saying that if he had done evil he was willing to confess and atone for it, Saul confessed he had done wickedly; and when David showed him the spear which he had taken from his side when he might have killed him Saul blessed him. But David did not believe in Saul's repentance, so he went with his six hundred men to a city of the Philistines called Ziklag, where he remained a year and four months.

At that time the Philistines made war against Saul, and he gathered all Israel together, and made his camp at Gilboa. And when he saw the host of the Philistines he was afraid, and inquired of the Lord what he should do, but because he had forsaken the way of the Lord he answered him not. Then Saul disguised himself and went to a woman of Endor, who had a familiar spirit that came when it was called, and asked that he might see the prophet Samuel. And the Lord sent the spirit of Samuel, for he was now dead. But Saul got no comfort from Samuel, for he told him that the Lord had departed from him, that his kingdom had been rent out of his hand and given to David, and that on the morrow the Philistines would conquer Israel, and that he and his sons would be slain. When Saul heard this news, he fell to the earth, and his strength left him. Then the woman gave him food, and he rose up and departed.

Next day the battle went against Saul, and the archers wounded him sorely, and Jonathan and two of his sons were killed. And Saul wished his armor-bearer to put him to death, but he was afraid; and the king, falling upon his own sword, fell dead. But David did not know of this great defeat at the time, for Achish, king of Gath, had sent him away from amongst the Philistines before the battle had begun. So David and his men went to Ziklag, where they found the place laid waste by the Amalekites. But David found where they were, and brought back the women and children, and all the spoil they had taken. And on the third day, a fugitive from Gilboa came and told David that Saul and Jonathan were slain. And David rent his clothes, and mourned and wept for Saul and Jonathan, and for the house of Israel.

CHAPTER X

DAVID MADE KING IN HEBRON—HIS SIN IN THE MATTER OF URIAH AND BATHSHEBA—HE IS REPROVED BY NATHAN THE PROPHET—THE BIRTH OF SOLOMON—THE REBELLION OF ABSALOM—DAVID'S DEATH—SOLOMON BUILDS THE TEMPLE—HIS DEATH—HE IS SUCCEEDED BY MANY WICKED KINGS.

DAVID now inquired of the Lord if he should go up into any of the cities of Judah. And the Lord told him to go to Hebron, the chief city of his own tribe; and the chief men gathered round him and made him their king. Thus was the prophecy fulfilled that the kingdom should be given to the tribe of Judah, for David belonged to that tribe.

After the death of Ish-bosheth, a son of Saul who ruled over a part of the kingdom, and who was slain contrary to the wishes of David, he went to live at Jerusalem, which henceforth was called the city of David.

David then asked of the Lord whether if he went up against the Philistines they would be delivered into his hand. And the Lord commanded him to go up, and he would be victorious. And David smote the Philistines from Geba unto Gazer.

And David again gathered together all the chosen men of Israel, thirty thousand, and went with them to bring the ark of the Lord from the house of Abinadab. And while it was being brought in a new cart, drawn by oxen, Uzzah, one of the sons of Abinadab, seeing it shake because of the roughness of the way, put forth his hand to steady it. And the anger of God was kindled against him for his want of reverence, and God smote him that he died. After this the ark rested for a time in the house of Obed-edom, and all his household was blessed because of it. When this was told to David he prepared a tent for the ark of God, and brought it up from the house of Obed-edom. But this time it was carried on the shoulders of the priests, and treated with greater reverence. David offered sacrifices to God, and he was so glad at heart that he danced before the ark; and the people shouted, and the trumpets were sounded. After the ark had been set in its place David offered burnt offerings and peace offerings, and blessed the people in the name of the Lord. And now that David dwelt in his own house, and the Lord had given him rest from all his enemies, the wish was in his heart to build a house for the ark of the Lord. But the prophet Nathan was commanded to go unto David and reveal to him that the son that should come after him would build a house for the Lord, and that the Lord would establish David's seed upon the throne forever.

After this time David fell into great sin. While his men were still at war with the heathen tribes he remained at Jerusalem; and on an evening as he walked on the house-top he saw a very beautiful woman, whom he wished to make his wife. He asked who she was, and was told that her name was Bathsheba, and that she was already the wife of one of his soldiers, a man named Uriah. Then David thought if Uriah were sent out of the way he might have Bathsheba to wife. So he sent a message to his captain Joab, to place Uriah in the fore-front of the battle, where he would likely be killed. Joab obeyed the order which he had received, and very soon afterwards a message came that Uriah the Hittite was slain.

But the Lord was displeased with David for what he had done, and Nathan the prophet came to him and told David a parable which brought home his guilt to him. Part of his punishment was to be that there would be perpetual warfare and strife in his own family. And David was stricken with sorrow, and said, I have sinned against the Lord. His punishment soon came, for the child that was born to him by her who had been the wife of Uriah sickened and died. While the child was ill David fasted and wept, but after its death he went to the tabernacle and worshipped God. Another son was born to David, who became the great king Solomon, the wisest man that ever lived.

Another part of David's punishment was the rebellion of his beautiful and beloved son Absalom, who caused his half-brother Amnon to be slain, and then fled from Jerusalem. After three years' exile from his father's house Absalom was allowed to return, and after a time was restored to his father's favor. But he soon set to work in a mean and crafty way to win the hearts of the people over to his service, in order that he might be made king; and he went out with a small army to Hebron pretending that he was going to offer sacrifices. When the news of Absalom's rebellion was brought to David he left Jerusalem with an army, in case his son should come up against it and take it. On their way a man of the family of Saul, named Shimei, cursed the king and his men, and threw stones at them. Meantime Absalom entered Jerusalem with his men, and asked advice from Ahithophel and Hushai, two of his father's counsellors. The advice of Ahithophel was to send a large army at once and capture his father, and so secure the throne for himself. But Hushai, who was friendly to David, counselled delay. Absalom took the advice of Hushai, and so in that way God turned the counsel of Ahithophel to foolishness. And when he saw that his advice was disregarded, he went and hanged himself.

Meantime David and his men had crossed the Jordan for safety, and reached the city of Mahanaim. And Absalom also passed over Jordan with a great army into the land of Gilead. And a battle took place in the wood of Ephraim, when the army of Absalom was completely routed. As he fled from the army of his father, the mule upon which he rode went under the boughs of an oak tree, so that Absalom's head was caught in the boughs, and he was left hanging there. And a certain man told Joab that Absalom was hanging from one of the trees of the forest. So Joab went and thrust him through with a dart as he hung there, and his body was cast into a pit in the wood, and stones were piled upon it. When the tidings were brought to David of the death of his son he was waiting between the two gates of Mahanaim. And when he heard the sad news, he went up to the chamber over the gate, and wept: and as he went, he said, O my son Absalom!

my son, my son Absalom! would God I had died for thee, O Absalom, my son, my son!

After this, David, tempted by Satan, caused the people to be numbered, and for this sin a pestilence was sent amongst them. While the destroying angel stood by the threshing-floor of Araunah, the Jebusite, ready to smite the people of Jerusalem, David beseeched the Lord that he himself should be punished, and the people spared. And Gad the prophet commanded David to rear an altar unto the Lord on the threshing-floor; and David did so, and the plague was stayed.

When David was old and well stricken in years, his son Adonijah rebelled against him, and taking into his counsel Joab the captain of the host and Abiathar the priest, put himself up for king. But David commanded that Solomon should be anointed king while he himself yet lived. And when this was done he sent for Solomon, and charged him to serve God with a perfect heart and with a willing mind, for if he sought God he would be found of him, but if he forsook him he would cast him off forever. And David gave to Solomon the pattern of the temple, and presented to him all the costly materials he had collected for the work. He also instructed him in the order of the service, as he had received it from the Lord, and gave him the courses of the priests and Levites. Then David blessed the Lord before all the congregation, and said, Blessed be thou, Lord God of Israel our father, for ever and ever. And he said to the congregation, Now bless the Lord your God. And all the congregation blessed the Lord God of their fathers, and worshipped

THE DEATH OF ABSALOM

the Lord. Then the people ate and drank that day with great gladness. And all the people submitted themselves unto Solomon, and he sat on the throne of David his father.

And David died, after having reigned as king for forty years; seven in Hebron, and thirty-three in Jerusalem.

Then Solomon sat upon the throne of David his father, and the Lord was with him and magnified him exceedingly. And he went up to Gibeon with all the congregation to sacrifice unto the Lord, and while there God appeared to him in a dream, and said to him, Ask what I shall give thee. And Solomon asked for an understanding heart, that he might go out and in before the people, and judge them wisely.

The wisdom of Solomon was exemplified in the way he dealt with two women who had quarrelled with one another as to which of them was the mother of a child. They lived in the same house, and the child of one of them having died, its mother took it and laid it beside the other woman, and took away the living child as her own. And they came before the king for him to decide their quarrel. And the king ordered that the living child should be divided in two, and a half given to each woman. Then the mother of the living child said, O my lord, give her the living child, and in no wise slay it. But the other said, Let it be divided. Then the king ordered that the living child should be given to the first, for he said, She is the mother thereof. And the people saw that the wisdom of God was in the king.

SOLOMON ANOINTED KING

Solomon now began to carry out the instructions of his father David for the building of the temple. Clever workmen were sent by Hiram, king of Tyre, to prepare the stones and the cedars of Lebanon for the building. And all the wood and stone was made ready before it was laid in their place, so that there was no noise heard while the temple was being built.

After four years of preparation the building was begun, the site chosen being on Mount Moriah, the place which David had chosen, and where Abraham many hundreds of years before had meant to offer up his son Isaac. And it took seven years to build. The plan of it was the same as that of the tabernacle. There was a holy place for the altar of incense, the table of shewbread, and the golden candlestick. In the holy of holies was placed the ark containing the tables of stone, overshadowed by the two cherubims. The whole building was adorned with gold and precious stones, and the wood-work was covered with gold. There was also a great altar and vessels of brass, all of the finest workmanship.

When it was finished, Solomon called a great assembly of the people for its dedication. And he knelt before the people on a platform of brass, and spreading forth his hands, prayed that the Lord would watch over the place by day and night, and hear the prayers that would be offered there. And if any one in distress cried upon God, Solomon beseeched that the Lord would hear in heaven, his dwelling-place, and when he heard that he would forgive. Now when Solomon had made an end of

THE QUEEN OF SHEBA VISITS KING SOLOMON

praying, fire came down from heaven and consumed the burnt-offering and the sacrifices. And after the dedication Solomon held a great feast, and afterwards the people returned to their homes, glad of heart for all the goodness the Lord had done for David and for Israel.

The Lord again appeared to Solomon in a dream, and told him that his prayer had been heard, and that he had chosen the temple for his place of sacrifice. If Solomon walked before him, as David had walked, and obeyed his commandments, his throne would be established, but if the king and the people forgot his commandments, and worshipped idols, then they would be driven out of their own land, and the beautiful house would be destroyed.

So Solomon prospered greatly, and built many cities, amongst them Tadmor, or Palmyra, in the desert. He had many ships, which brought him gold from Ophir, and silver, ivory and many beautiful things from other countries. And his fame spread abroad, for he was wiser than any man that had ever lived before. The Book of Proverbs contains some of his wise sayings; he also wrote several Psalms, the Book of Ecclesiastes, and the Song of Solomon. The Queen of Sheba heard of his fame, and came to see him, bringing with her spices, gold and precious stones as presents. When she saw his wealth, the number of his servants and his rich clothing, and heard his great wisdom, she was astonished, and said that the half had not been told to her.

But notwithstanding Solomon's wisdom he fell into grievous sin. He married many wives, who

SOLOMON RETURNS TO IDOLATRY

worshipped strange gods, and they turned Solomon's heart astray after their gods. And the Lord was angry with him, and told him that because of this sin the kingdom would be taken away from his son, and he would be left with only one tribe to reign over. Another king was to rule over the other ten tribes; and henceforward there would be two kingdoms—Judah and Israel. Many adversaries rose up against Solomon in his last days; and he died, and his son Rehoboam reigned in his stead.

Rehoboam was a proud and headstrong man, and as was foretold to Solomon, only the tribe of Judah remained faithful to him. Jeroboam, the son of one of Solomon's household, was chosen king over the other ten tribes. And Rehoboam made an attempt to recover the rest of the kingdom, but being warned by the Lord he desisted. Jeroboam, who ruled over Israel, chose Ephraim as his chief city, and in order to keep the people from going up to Jerusalem to worship, he set up a golden calf in Bethel, and another in Dan, which led them into idolatry. A prophet from the tribe of Judah warned Jeroboam that there would arise a king in Judah who would punish his false prophets for their wickedness.

Rehoboam, the king of Judah, ruled his people wisely for three years, and walked in the way of David and Solomon. But at the end of that time he led the people into idolatry. For this cause, Shishak, king of Egypt, was allowed to come up against Jerusalem, and he carried away much of the treasures and precious things from the temple, and from the king's house. And there was continual warfare between Rehoboam the king of Judah and Jeroboam the king of Israel, until the death of the former, when his son Abijah reigned in his stead and overcame Jeroboam. After Abijah came Asa, and then Jehoshaphat. Meantime there had been in Israel six evil kings, and the sixth, Ahab, was the worst of them all. His wife Jezebel encouraged him in his evil, and he worshipped idols. During this reign Israel was sunk in idolatry, and those who served the true God were hunted and put to death. But Obadiah, one of Ahab's servants, being a good man, hid a hundred of the prophets of the Lord in a cave to save them from the persecution of Jezebel.

CHAPTER XI

ELIJAH THE PROPHET REPROVES AHAB—THE PROPHETS OF BAAL SLAIN IN MOUNT CARMEL—ELIJAH TAKEN UP TO HEAVEN—ELISHA SUCCEEDS HIM—NAAMAN THE SYRIAN—AHAB AND JEZEBEL SLAIN—THE END OF THE KINGDOM OF JUDAH—THE STORY OF JOB.

AND God sent the prophet Elijah to warn King Ahab that because of his wickedness a great drought would come upon Israel, and that there would be neither dew nor rain for three years. After delivering his message Elijah went to live beside the brook Cherith, where the ravens brought him bread and flesh in the morning, and bread and flesh in the evening. And he drank of the brook. When the brook was dry, at God's command Elijah went to the city of Zarephath, to the house of a widow. This woman had only a handful of meal in a barrel and a little oil; and when Elijah came she was gathering a few sticks to make a fire whereon to cook a last meal for herself and her son before they died. Then Elijah told her that her meal and oil would last in a miraculous manner until the Lord sent rain upon the earth; and this happened as Elijah had said. After this the widow's son fell sick and died. And Elijah took the body and laid it upon his own bed, and stretched himself three times upon it, and prayed earnestly that God would bring the child back to life; and the Lord heard his prayer, and the child's soul came again. Then the widow knew assuredly that a man of God had been living under her roof.

After the three years of drought, Elijah went to see King Ahab. And the king said to him, Art thou he that troubleth Israel? And Elijah said, I have not troubled Israel, but thou hast, in that thou hast followed Baalim. And Elijah asked Ahab to call together all Israel and the priests of Baal and Ashtaroth to Mount Carmel. And when they were gathered there, Elijah said to the people, How long halt ye between two opinions? If the Lord be God, follow him; but if Baal, then follow him. Then Elijah caused two sacrifices to be prepared, one for himself, and one for the prophets of Baal, and neither of them was to put fire below their offering; but, said Elijah to the prophets of Baal, Call ye on the name of your gods, and I will call on the name of the Lord; and the God that answereth by fire let

ELIJAH FED BY RAVENS

him be the God. Then the prophets of Baal called from morning till night, O Baal, hear us! But there was neither voice nor answer. At this Elijah mocked them, and asked the people to come near to him. Then, alone there to witness for the God of Israel before hundreds of idolaters, he repaired a ruined altar, and caused a trench to be made round it. Then he laid wood and a bullock upon the altar, and water was poured over the sacrifice and into the trench. And at the time of the evening sacrifice Elijah prayed to God that he would let it be known that he was God, and that Elijah was his servant, so that the hearts of the people might be turned again towards him. Then fire fell from heaven, and burned the sacrifice and the altar, and dried up the water in the trench. When the people saw this, they fell on their faces, saying, The Lord he is the God; the Lord he is the God. And the false prophets of Baal were taken down to the brook Kishon and slain there. When Ahab told his wife Jezebel how Elijah had slain the prophets of Baal, she determined to slay him. And he fled to the wilderness, and was sleeping under a juniper-tree, when the angel of the Lord touched him, and bade him arise and eat. And Elijah looked and saw a cake baked upon the coals beside him, and a cruse of water standing by. And he arose and did eat and drink and was strengthened. After that he journeyed to Horeb, and went into a cave there. And the Lord asked him, What doest thou here, Elijah? And Elijah answered that it was because the men of Israel had forsaken the true God, and he only was left. And the Lord commanded him to return toward the wilderness of Damascus, and anoint Elisha the prophet to succeed him. Elisha was ploughing with his oxen in the field when Elijah came near and threw his mantle over him. And Elisha went with him, and became his servant.

After this Ahab coveted the vineyard of a man named Naboth at Jezreel. And Jezebel, finding that Ahab was sad because he could not get it by purchase from Naboth, sent and had the owner put to death. Because of this Elijah warned him that evil would be sent upon him, for the dogs would lick his blood in the place where they licked the blood of Naboth; and of Jezebel, he said that the dogs would eat her by the wall of Jezreel. And so it happened, for Ahab was wounded in battle with Ben-hadad; and as his chariot was being washed in the pool of Samaria the dogs came and licked his blood from it.

When the time came for the Lord to take Elijah into heaven, he went with Elisha to Gilgal. And he wanted to be alone, but Elisha would not leave him, so they went to Bethel together. At Bethel the young men in the schools of the prophets said to Elisha, Knowest thou that the Lord will take away thy master from thy head to-day? Elisha answered, Yea, I know it: hold ye your peace. And they went on to Jericho, and the same question was put to Elisha there by the young prophets, and they received the same answer. Elijah still entreated his servant to leave him, but Elisha said, As the Lord liveth, and as thy soul liveth, I will not leave thee. So they went on to Jordan, and Elijah smote the waters with his mantle, and they passed over on dry ground. And as they walked and talked together, Elijah asked Elisha what he should do for him before he was taken away; and Elisha asked that a double portion of Elijah's spirit might rest upon him. Elijah said, Thou hast asked a hard thing; but if thou see me taken from thee, it shall be so; if not, it shall not be so. And as they still went on and talked, there came a chariot of fire, and horses of fire, and parted them asunder, and Elijah went up to heaven. And when Elisha saw this he cried out, My father, my father! the chariots of Israel and the horsemen thereof. And he rent his own clothes, and took up the mantle of Elijah which had fallen from him.

Among the many miraculous things that Elisha did was the following: There dwelt in the city of Shunem a great woman, who was very kind to Elisha, and every time he passed that way he turned in thither to eat bread. And she and her husband set apart a little room in their house for the use of the prophet. Now this woman had no children, but Elisha promised her that by and by she should have a son. And it happened according to Elisha's word, for a son was born to her. And one day, when the boy had grown up, he was out in the fields with the reapers, and he complained of his head. He was taken home and laid on his mother's knees, and at noon he died. His mother then laid him on the bed of the prophet, and saddled an ass and went in great haste to Mount Carmel to seek Elisha. And when she told the prophet what had happened, he had compassion upon her, and sent his servant Gehazi to touch the child's face with his staff; but

ELIJAH TAKEN UP TO HEAVEN IN A CHARIOT

the child showed no signs of life. When Elisha came he prayed to the Lord that the child might be restored to life again, and he lay down upon the child, and stretched himself upon him, and he became warm, sneezed seven times, and came to life.

Now Naaman, the captain of the army of the Syrians, was a great man with his master, and an honorable and very valiant; but he was a leper. And there was a little maid in waiting on his wife who had been brought away as a captive from the land of Israel; and she was sorry for the distress of her master. So she made bold to tell her mistress of the man of God called Elisha, who lived in her native country, and said she was sure he would be able to cure her master Naaman. After much persuasion Naaman went to the house of Elisha. But the prophet sent a message to the proud Syrian captain that if he went and washed in the river Jordan seven times he would be clean. And Naaman was angry when he heard this, and said he thought the prophet would have come and touched him, and so have freed him from his leprosy at once. He asked if Abana and Pharpar, rivers in his own country, were not better than all the rivers in Israel. But his servants reasoned with him, and said if the prophet had asked him to do some great thing, would he not have done it? how much more, then, when he only said to him, Wash and be clean! So Naaman went at last, and dipped himself in the Jordan, and his flesh became clean as that of a little child. And he went to Elisha, and said, Behold, now I know that there is no God in all the earth but in Israel. And he offered a present to Elisha, but the prophet would receive nothing from his hand. And Gehazi, the servant of Elisha, acted deceitfully, for he ran after Naaman, and received a present from him, saying it was for his master. Then Elisha told Gehazi that as a punishment the leprosy of Naaman should cleave to him and to all his descendants forever.

While the king of Syria was troubling Israel, and sending out bands of soldiers into the country, the king of Israel was continually forewarned as to where they were by Elisha. And some one told the king of Syria how the army of Israel came to know all their movements, so he sent chariots and horsemen to Dothan, where the prophet was, to take him. Next morning Elisha's servant saw the great host of the Syrians, and told his master. Elisha bade him fear not; for those that were with them were more than those that were against them. And Elisha prayed that his servant's eyes might be opened, when lo, he saw the mountain full of horses and chariots of fire round about Elisha. When the Syrian horsemen and chariots came towards Elisha to take him, he prayed to the Lord, and said, Smite this people with blindness. And the Lord smote them with blindness, according to the word of Elisha. Then Elisha led them to Samaria, where they became the captives of the king of Israel, who dealt kindly with them, and sent them back to the Syrian camp.

On another occasion, when there was a great famine in Samaria because of its being besieged by the king of Syria, the people were miraculously provided for. The Lord caused the Syrians to hear the noise of chariots and horses, and thus made them fly and leave all their spoil behind them, which fell into the hands of the Israelites. Four lepers who had been cast outside the city gate were the first to discover that the Syrian camp was deserted, and brought word into Samaria.

And now the word of Elijah, which he spoke regarding the wicked Jezebel, was fulfilled. Jehu had slain Jehoram, the son of Ahab, near Jezreel. On passing through the city Jehu made a sign to those in Jezebel's house who were on his side; and Jezebel, who was seated at a window, was cast down at Jehu's command, and the horses of his chariot trod her under foot. Shortly afterwards Jehu sent to bury her body, for he said she was a king's daughter, but they found only her bones, because the dogs had eaten her flesh. And Jehu sent word to the inhabitants of Samaria commanding them to slay Ahab's seventy sons who were there. And they slew them, and sent their heads to Jehu at Jezreel. And Jehu himself slew all that were in Jezreel of Ahab's house, and his great men and his priests, until he left none remaining.

During the reign of Jeroboam over Israel the cities of Damascus and Hamath were taken from the Syrians. But the people became idolaters, and forgot to serve God, and continued to worship golden calves. The prophets Amos and Hosea both proclaimed to the king and the people that greater punishments would come upon them in the future than had ever been in the past, for an enemy would come and take them captive, and treat them with cruelty. Ever since Israel had been made a king-

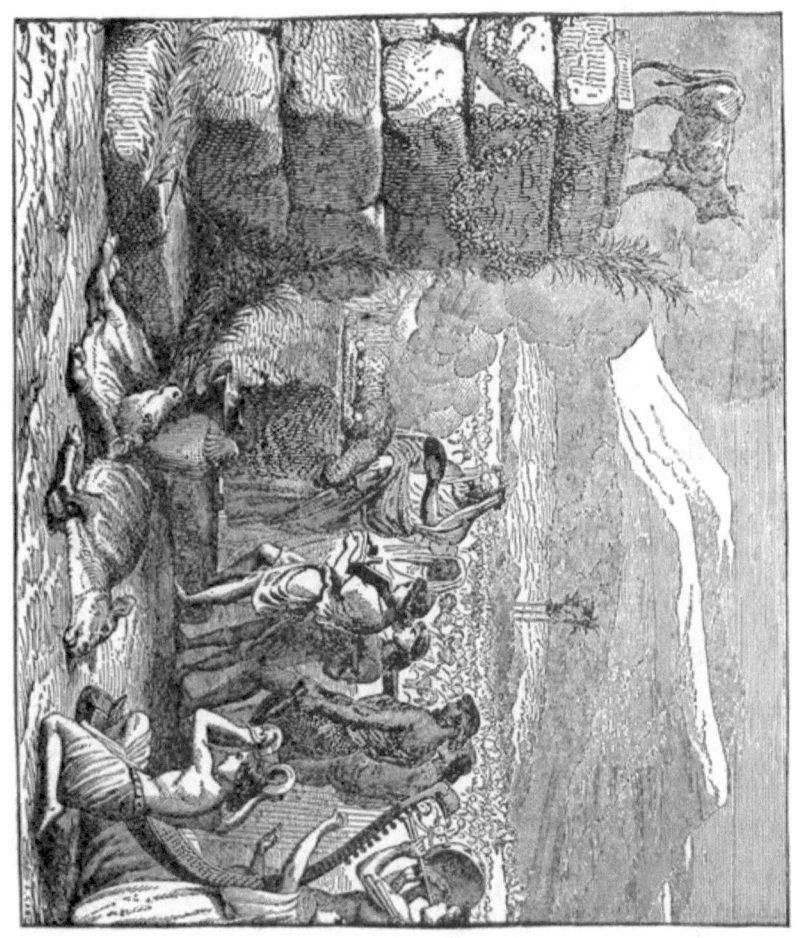
WORSHIPPING THE GOLDEN CALF

dom the kings and the people had departed from the commandments of God, and had worshipped the false gods which were set up in the high places. Since Jeroboam had been chosen king two hundred and fifty-four years had passed, and nineteen kings had ruled over them, all of whom had done wickedly. So what the prophets had foretold came to pass. The king of Assyria came into the land of Israel, and taking the people captive, he gave them cities to live in, but would not allow them to return to their own country. We do not know what became of the ten tribes after they were taken captive into Assyria; but the king of that land sent his own people to dwell in the cities of Israel. We read that the Lord was very angry with Israel, and removed them out of his sight; there was none left but the tribe of Judah only. Of the land given to Israel only the kingdom of Judah remained, and good Hezekiah was king there at that time. And Samaria was colonized by the heathen people.

The kingdom of Judah ended in this way. While Jehoiachin reigned in Jerusalem, Nebuchadnezzar, king of Babylon, came and spoiled the temple and the king's palace, and also took the king, his mother, his wives, and the princes of Judah, and the soldiers in Jerusalem, captive to Babylon. And there they remained for seventy years; and Jeremiah the prophet wrote a letter, and bade them be contented, as Jerusalem was to be destroyed. The prophet Ezekiel, instructed by signs and visions, also told them the same thing.

And Nebuchadnezzar made Zedekiah king of Jerusalem, but he rebelled against him. Jeremiah prophesied that Jerusalem would fall into the hands of the king of Babylon, and for this he was let down into a deep pit; but the king afterwards commanded that he should be drawn out. Jeremiah told the king if he would go out and deliver himself up to the king of Babylon, he would be saved alive, and the city would not be burned with fire. But Zedekiah disregarded the command of the Lord, and the city was besieged for eighteen months. And when he attempted to escape he was caught by the Chaldeans; his two sons were killed before his eyes, his eyes were put out, and he was carried captive to Babylon, where he died in prison. The temple was burned at this time by the captain of Nebuchadnezzar's army, the city walls were broken down, and the people of Jerusalem who were not slain were carried away captive to Babylon.

Thus ended the kingdom of Judah, after lasting for about three hundred and eighty-eight years, nineteen kings and one queen having reigned since Rehoboam the son of Solomon was made king over the tribes of Judah and Benjamin. But now, because of their disobedience against God, they were carried away captive to another country.

In very early times in Bible history there lived a wealthy man in the land of Uz, named Job, who was blessed of God, because he served him with a perfect heart. But one day Satan appeared before God, and accused Job of only serving him for selfish reasons. If he were to deprive him of all the good things which he had, then Job would serve him no longer.

And God gave Satan power over Job to tempt

him, only his life was to be spared. And now disaster after disaster came upon this servant of God. While his seven sons and daughters were feasting together at their eldest brother's house, a messenger came to him, and told him that his enemies had killed his servants in the fields, and taken away his oxen and asses. Then another came and said that his sheep and shepherds had been killed by lightning. Still another came and told him that the Chaldeans had slain more of his servants, and stolen all his camels. Last of all came one and said that a wind from heaven had smitten his eldest son's house, and the house had fallen and killed his children. Then Job rent his clothes, and fell upon the ground, and worshipped. He answered, The Lord gave, and the Lord hath taken away ; blessed be the name of the Lord. In all this Job sinned not, nor charged God foolishly.

And again Satan received permission from God to afflict Job, and see if he could not make him sin. This time he was smitten with sore boils from head to foot. When his wife saw him thus afflicted, she said to him, Dost thou still retain thine integrity? curse God and die. Job rebuked her for her folly, and said, Shall we receive good at the hand of God, and shall we not receive evil? Three of his friends came to mourn with him, and to comfort him in his trouble. And they sat on the ground with Job seven days and seven nights, and none spake to him, for they saw that his grief was very great. Then Job opened his mouth, cursing the day of his birth, and wishing for death. And his friends reasoned with him, and tried to show him that his troubles had come on him because of his sins. Job, in return, acknowledged God's justice, and expressed his confidence in him, but reproving his friends for partiality, and complained of their cruelty. Then Elihu, another friend of Job, reproved both him and his three friends. And the Lord answered Job, and Job humbled himself; and God commanded his friends to offer up for themselves a burnt-offering, and Job would pray for them, for he had accepted Job, who had spoken of him the thing that was right.

And God restored Job to health again, and made him even richer in servants and cattle than he had been before. His friends brought him presents; and seven more sons and daughters were born to him, who were even more beautiful than those he had lost. And Job lived, after the return of his prosperity, one hundred and forty years.

CHAPTER XII

THE STORY OF JONAH AND NINEVEH—NEBUCHADNEZZAR SETS UP AN IMAGE—THE THREE YOUNG HEBREWS IN THE FIERY FURNACE—DANIEL IN THE DEN OF LIONS—THE STORY OF ESTHER—THE TEMPLE REBUILT.

IN the reign of Jehu, king of Israel, there lived a prophet of the Lord named Jonah, and he was sent by God to warn the inhabitants of the great Assyrian city, Nineveh, that unless they repented he would destroy the city, for their wickedness had come up before him. But Jonah was afraid to deliver the message of warning; and instead, he went down to the seaport of Joppa, and took passage there in a ship for his own country. And a great storm broke over the ship, and the sailors, who were heathens, began to cry upon their gods to help them. The master of the ship, finding Jonah asleep, bade him arise, and, like them, call upon his God. Then the sailors, believing that this trouble had come upon them because of some one in the ship, cast lots, and the lot fell upon Jonah. And they asked him who he was, and Jonah replied that he was a Hebrew and a worshipper of the God of heaven, entreating them at the same time to cast him overboard, as he knew that God had sent the storm because of him. Now they were unwilling to do so, but as the storm did not abate, they prayed to the Lord not to lay innocent blood to their charge; and they cast Jonah into the sea, and immediately it became calm. Then the sailors worshipped the Lord, who had brought them deliverance. And a great fish was prepared, which swallowed Jonah; and he remained three days and three nights in the belly of the fish, praying to God. Then the fish cast Jonah out upon the dry land. And the word of the Lord came to Jonah a second time to go up to Nineveh. So Jonah went and proclaimed to the people of Nineveh that unless they repented, in forty days the city would be destroyed.

And the king and the people of Nineveh believed God, and, repenting of their wickedness, he had compassion on them. But Jonah was not pleased because God had been merciful and had spared the city; so he went and made himself a cool arbor outside the walls, where he could see if the judgment he had spoken of would come to pass. As Jonah sat there a vine grew up in a single night, and afforded him a pleasant shade from the heat of the sun. But next morning a worm destroyed the vine, and made it wither, which caused Jonah to be angry. And God asked him if he did well to be angry about so small a matter. And Jonah said, I do well to be angry even unto death. And God said to him, surely if he had pity on a plant which sprang up in a night and perished in a night, much more ought he to have pity on Nineveh, wherein were so many people, and thousands of them children.

At the time when Nebuchadnezzar, king of Babylon, took captive Jehoiakim, king of Judah, and carried him away to Babylon, with the treasures of the house of God, he ordered the chief servant of his household to look out certain of the young Israelites to wait on him in his palace, and to be instructed in all the learning of the Chaldeans. They were to have daily provision from the king's table, and to drink of the king's wine. But four of these young men, named Shadrach, Meshach, Abednego and Daniel, would not eat the meat or drink the wine, because it had been offered to idols. So Daniel and his friends got permission from the steward who was set over them to live on vegetable food for ten days, and to drink water only. At the end of that time they were fairer and fatter than the other young men who ate from the king's table.

And God gave these youths knowledge and skill in all learning and wisdom; so much was this the case, that when they were brought before Nebuchadnezzar he found that amongst his servants none were equal to Daniel and his three friends. Now the king dreamed a dream, and when he awoke it had passed from him, and he asked the wise men of Babylon to tell him his dream, and the intepretation of it. And when they could not, the king was angry, and ordered that they should all be slain. When Daniel heard of this, he sent word to the king that if time were given him he would relate the dream and give the interpretation. And Daniel and his three friends prayed to the Lord, and he showed Daniel the dream and its interpretation. And Daniel, when he stood before the king, told him that it was not because he was wiser than any one else that he was able to interpret the dream, but because God had showed it to him. Then he declared to the king as follows:

The image which Nebuchadnezzar had seen in his dream had a head of fine gold, the breast and arms were of silver, the belly and the thighs of brass, and the feet were part iron and part clay. A stone cut out of a mountain, without hands, came and struck the feet of the image, dashing them to pieces, and causing it to fall, and it was broken into dust, which the wind blew away. The head of gold meant Nebuchadnezzar's kingdom, which was the greatest in the world at the time; while the silver, brass, iron, and clay meant other and lesser kingdoms which should arise after he was dead. The stone meant an everlasting kingdom which the God of heaven would set up, and which would never be destroyed.

Nebuchadnezzar afterwards made an image of gold, and sent for all the chief men in his kingdom, and proclaimed to them that as soon as they heard the sound of music they were to fall down and worship this image, and whoever did not fall down and worship it would be cast into a burning fiery furnace. But Shadrach, Meshach, and Abed-nego, whom the king had made rulers, did not obey the summons; and accordingly they were bound in their coats and hats and cast into the burning fiery furnace. And the furnace was so hot that the men who cast them in were burned. But although these three captives fell bound into the fire, they soon rose up, and were seen by the king walking in the fire. And he was astonished at this strange sight, and said to his rulers, Did not we cast three men bound into the fire? They answered and said, True, O king! And the king said, Lo, I see four men loose, walking in the midst of the fire, and the form of the fourth is like to the Son of God. And the king went to the mouth of the furnace, and called upon them to come out; and when Shadrach, Meshach, and Abed-nego came out, the smell of fire had not passed upon them. After this the king blessed their God, and made a decree that no one should speak evil of them, and promoted them to greater dignity than before.

After this Nebuchadnezzar dreamed again. He beheld in his dream a great, tall, wide-spreading tree, the leaves whereof were fair and the fruit much; and a holy watcher came down from heaven, and ordered the tree to be cut down, and its leaves and fruit to be scattered, but the stump was to be left in the earth, and it was to be wet with the dew of heaven. Then Daniel interpreted the dream to the king, and told him that it shadowed forth what was to befall himself. He was to be driven forth from men, and made to eat grass like the oxen, and would be wet with the dew of heaven until he learned that the Most High ruled over all. When twelve months had passed, all this befell the king. He was driven into the fields, where he ate grass like an ox, and his body was wet with the dew. After seven years his understanding returned, and he blessed the Most High, whose dominion is an everlasting dominion, and his kingdom from generation to generation.

After Nebuchadnezzar's death, Belshazzar his son reigned in his stead. And he held a great feast, with a thousand of his lords, and he commanded that the golden vessels should be brought which his father had taken from the temple at Jerusalem, in order to drink wine from them. So they drank wine, and praised their idols of gold, silver, iron, wood and stone. As they feasted, there came the hand of a man, and wrote an inscription upon the wall, which caused the king's face to change, and his heart to be filled with fear. None of the wise men could interpret the writing until Daniel was called, and he told the king that because he was high and lifted up, and had forgotten God, the inscription, MENE, MENE, TEKEL, UPHARSIN, meant that God had taken the kingdom from him and given it to the Medes and Persians. Then Belshazzar commanded that Daniel should be clothed in scarlet, and have a gold chain round his neck, and should be proclaimed the third ruler in the kingdom.

That same night Darius the Median took the kingdom, slew Belshazzar, and reigned in his stead.

It pleased Darius to make Daniel the first of the three presidents who were over the hundred and twenty princes of his kingdom. But the others hated him, and tried to find occasion against him before the king. But they could find nothing against him, except concerning the law of his God. So they persuaded the king to sign a decree, that whosoever should ask a petition of any god or man for thirty days, except from the king, should be cast into a den of lions. But when Daniel knew that the decree was signed, he went into his house, and the windows of his chamber being open toward Jerusalem, he kneeled upon his knees, and prayed and gave thanks to God three times a day. Then his accusers went and told the king. When the king heard this he was displeased with himself, and set his heart to deliver Daniel. But the decree could not be changed, and Darius commanded that Daniel should be cast into the den of lions, but said to him, Thy God, whom thou servest continually, will deliver thee. And a large stone was laid upon the mouth of the den.

Darius went home to his palace depressed in spirit, and passed the night fasting. And early next morning he came to the den of lions, and cried with a lamentable voice, asking Daniel if the God in whom he trusted had delivered him. And Daniel replied, O king, live forever. My God hath sent his angel, and hath shut the lions' mouths, that they have not hurt me, because I have not sinned against him; and also unto thee, O king, I have done no wrong. And the king commanded that Daniel should be brought forth. And the men who had spoken against him were cast into the den of lions, with their wives and children; and immediately they were torn in pieces.

In the first year of the reign of Darius, Daniel, understanding from the words of Jeremiah the prophet that the seventy years of captivity were nearly accomplished, set his face to seek the Lord God by prayer and supplication, confession of the sins of his people, and fasting. And while he was praying, the angel Gabriel touched him at the time of the evening oblation, and revealed to him that the Jews would be allowed to return to their own land, and build up Jerusalem, and that in about four hundred and eighty-three years afterwards the Messiah would be born.

At the end of the seventy years the Lord stirred up the spirit of Cyrus, king of Persia, to permit the Jews to return to their own country. And the priests and Levites, and the men amongst the Jews whom the Lord had made willing, prepared to return to Jerusalem to rebuild the house of God; and Cyrus gave back the vessels of the temple to Zerubbabel, a prince of Judah. Over forty thousand persons returned at this time. They found Jerusalem in ruins, and the first thing they did was to rebuild the altar of the Lord, and offer the

DANIEL IN THE LIONS' DEN

appointed sacrifices thereon. They also began to rebuild the temple; but they were stopped because of the false report sent to Artaxerxes, the successor of Cyrus. It was finished, however, in the reign of Artaxerxes' successor.

While Ahasuerus ruled in Persia there were still many Jews living amongst his people who had not returned to Jerusalem. And in the third year of his reign the king made a great feast unto all his princes and servants, and he sent for his queen Vashti to come to the feast, with the crown upon her head, that his guests might see her beauty.

But the queen refused to come; and when the king took counsel of his wise men, they recommended that Vashti should come no more before the king, and that her royal estate should be given to another better than she. Now among the servants of the palace there was one Mordecai, a Jew, who had been the means of saving the king's life, and he had a very fair and beautiful cousin named Esther. Her he brought under the notice of the king, and she was chosen to be queen by Ahasuerus instead of Vashti. And the king had another servant named Haman, whom Mordecai had offended by not bowing down to him. Now Haman was full of wrath at Mordecai, but he scorned to lay hands on him alone, but sought rather to slay all the Jews that were in the land. So he sought the king's permission to make a decree that all the Jews should be destroyed, offering, if it were granted to him, to put ten thousand talents of silver into the king's treasury. The king gave Haman permission to do to the Jews as it seemed good to him; and it was ordered that on a certain day the Persians were to fall upon the Jews, kill them, and take all their possessions to themselves. And copies of the decree were sent throughout Persia to all the rulers and governors. Now when Mordecai heard this he clothed himself in sackcloth, and mourned and wept, and sent a message to Queen Esther to intercede with the king on behalf of the Jews.

Then Esther bethought her of a plan to save her people. Although there was a law that whoever approached the king unasked should be put to death, yet Esther dressed herself in her royal robes, and went in and stood before him in the inner palace. And the king looked favorably upon her, and asked what was her request, for he would grant it even to the half of his kingdom. Then the queen requested that the king and Haman should come that day to a banquet which she had made ready for them. The king consented, and Haman went to the banquet with a proud heart. The queen invited the king and Haman to another feast next day. But before going to the feast Haman caused a gallows to be erected, intending to ask the king that Mordecai might be hanged upon it. On the following night, the king, being sleepless, caused the records of the kingdom to be read to him, and it was found written therein that Mordecai had warned him of a plot against his life. And on inquiring of his servants he found that Mordecai received no reward for the great service performed by him.

Next day, when Haman came before the king, he asked him what should be done to the man whom the king delighted to honor. Haman, thinking Ahasuerus meant himself, said, Let the royal apparel be put upon that man, and let him ride upon the king's horse, led by one of the princes. So the king ordered Haman to prepare at once to do this honor to Mordecai the Jew. And Mordecai was led in state through the streets of the city, dressed in the royal robes, sitting on the king's horse, and with a crown upon his head. After this honor Mordecai sat down again in his place at the king's gate; but Haman went home mourning because of the honor done to his enemy.

When the king and Haman were again seated at Esther's banquet, Ahasuerus asked what was her request. For answer she asked that her own life and the lives of her people might be given to her; for a decree had been issued that she and her people should be killed. The king asked who it was, and where he was, who had presumed to do this thing. Esther said, The adversary and the enemy is this wicked Haman. And the king was wroth, and caused Haman to be hanged on the gallows that he had prepared for Mordecai; and Mordecai was made ruler in the king's house in place of Haman. Another decree was sent out over all the land, granting to the Jews power, in the day in which the slaughter was to take place, to meet together and defend themselves against all who should rise against them.

Ninety years after Zerubbabel had gone down from Persia to Jerusalem, a Jew named Nehemiah, who was cupbearer to Artaxerxes, received permission from that king to go down to Jerusalem and repair

THE ISRAELITES RETURNING TO JERUSALEM

its ruined walls. And he found many enemies there who hindered him in his work, so that while half of the men of Israel worked on the wall, the other half had to defend the workers with swords, spears and bows. Those who were building also carried swords with them, and a trumpeter was stationed near them to warn the builders of the approach of any hostile person. When the wall was built, Sanballat and Tobiah, and other enemies of the Jews, were wroth, and they tempted Nehemiah to come out without the wall and speak with them. But Nehemiah refused, and thus their plans against the Jews were defeated. The wall was finished in fifty-two days, after which it was dedicated to the Lord by the priests, Levites, and the people. And Nehemiah ordered that the religious feasts appointed by Moses should be kept. But soon the people forgot the Lord; and when Nehemiah came back from Persia, whither he had gone, he found that the Jews had married heathen wives, were breaking the Sabbath, and neglecting to maintain their religious services. So Nehemiah warned them of the dangers into which they had fallen, and showed them that they were committing the same sin for which their fathers had been punished in the wilderness.

There was now a remnant of the people of Israel in their own land awaiting the coming of the Messiah. The prophets who uttered God's message to them, and also spoke of the coming of Christ, were Isaiah, Jeremiah, Ezekiel, Daniel and twelve others, ending with Malachi, who, being last, is called the "Seal of the Prophets." A collection of poems, praise songs, or psalms, some of them written by Moses and Solomon, but mostly by David, was also in the possession of the Jews at this time, and has been the prized heritage of the Church as an aid in prayer and praise through all the ages. David, assisted by the musician Asaph, seems first to have gathered these Psalms together to be sung in the temple service. Probably Ezra, who is supposed, when he settled in his own land, to have gathered together most of the books of the Old Testament, also completed the collection of Psalms as we have them now.

For over four hundred years we hear no more about the history of the Jews from the Bible. But we know from other books something about the people of the kingdom of Judah: that they remained servants to the king of Persia for about a hundred years after the time that Nehemiah returned from Babylon. Even while Nehemiah lived the Samaritans had erected on Mount Gerizim (near Samaria) a rival temple to that of the Jews at Jerusalem. Alexander the Great, on his way to conquer the whole East, took Jerusalem, and carried away a great number of the Jews to Egypt in order to people Alexandria. Ptolemy, one of his generals, who became king of Egypt, invaded Syria, took Jerusalem about three hundred years before the coming of Christ, and carried off about a hundred thousand of the people to settle in Alexandria and Cyrene. The Jews gained a great deal of refinement and learning from their Greek conquerors. But under one of the Egyptian kings the temple of Jerusalem was dedicated to the worship of false gods, and all the national feelings of the

Jews were outraged. The yoke of the Syrians, to whom they were afterwards subject, was broken, chiefly by the Jews led by the brave family of Mattathia and Judas Maccabæus. The brothers of the latter after his death completed the ascendency of the Jews, and established the Sanhedrim, or Jewish religious council. Two brothers disputing for ascendency as to who should be king, led to the interference of the Romans, who made Judea dependent on the Roman province of Syria. One of the governors of Galilee, named Herod, a fierce and cruel man, by the help of the Romans, conquered Jerusalem thirty-seven years before the birth of Christ. After ruling about eighteen years, to conciliate the people, he rebuilt the temple upon Mount Moriah. But there was no ark now to put in the holy place; most likely it was lost during the captivity. Outside Herod's temple, which glittered with plates of brass, gold and silver, there was a court called the Court of the Gentiles, which had nine large and beautiful gates, the finest of which was called the Beautiful Gate.

[All the history and biography in the Old Testament is but an introduction to the New Testament, and points forward towards, and prepares the way for, the coming of Christ, the Saviour of the world.]

REBUILDING THE TEMPLE AT JERUSALEM

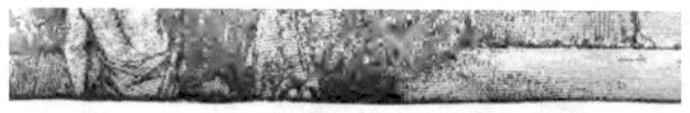

THE STORY
Of the New Testament

CHAPTER I

PALESTINE AT THE BIRTH OF OUR LORD—THE FORERUNNER—THE ANNUNCIATION TO MARY—THE SAVIOUR BORN IN BETHLEHEM—HEROD SLAYS THE YOUNG CHILDREN—THE FLIGHT INTO EGYPT—THE PREACHING OF JOHN—BAPTISM OF THE CHRIST.

PALESTINE, at the time when our Lord was born, was divided into three provinces.

Judea lay to the south, with its capital, Jerusalem, the holy city, where stood the temple, to which the people resorted three times a year to hold the solemn feasts ordained by the law of Moses. It has been estimated that at the passover three millions of people thronged the streets of Jerusalem, most of whom came up to offer sacrifices, for in no other place could sacrifices be offered to the God of Israel.

In the north lay Galilee, with its interesting lake, where our Lord lived for so many years, and did so many mighty works. Between those two districts lay Samaria, inhabited by a race descended from a heathen colony, who had largely intermarried with the Jews, but between whom and the Jews the most bitter enmity existed.

The prosperity of the descendants of the patriarchs had now come to an end. They were under the Roman yoke, and much discontent prevailed among them because of the heavy taxes they had to pay. Many a devout heart was longing and praying for the coming of the Messiah, the Deliverer. The popular idea was that he would come as a mighty king, able to conquer all his enemies, and keep them under; not many were prepared to welcome the lowly child Jesus as the Saviour of the world.

At this time, when Herod reigned over Judea, there lived a priest called Zacharias, and his wife's name was Elizabeth. They were both righteous before God, walking in all the commandments and ordinances of the Lord, blameless. And they had no children. Now Zacharias was in the temple burning incense, according to the custom of the priest's office, when an angel appeared unto him. He was at first afraid, but the angel bade him fear not; and told him that God would one day give him a son, who was to be called John, meaning, The Lord is gracious. His parents would have joy and gladness at his birth, and not only they, but many more would rejoice thereat. He was to be a Nazarite —that is, he was to drink neither wine nor strong drink—and he was to be filled with the Holy Spirit.

Zacharias did not at first believe the good news, and when he asked for a sign the angel told him that he was Gabriel, who stood in the presence of the Lord, and was sent to tell him these glad tidings;

THE ANNUNCIATION

and also that because of his unbelief, he should be unable to speak until the child was born.

The people who were praying in the outer court of the temple wondered why the priest did not come out, but when he did come, and was unable to speak, they knew he had seen a vision.

About six months after this the angel Gabriel was sent from God, on a similar errand, to a village in Galilee called Nazareth, to Mary, the espoused wife of a man called Joseph. They were poor people, but both of them belonged to the house of David.

The angel came in unto Mary, and said, Hail, thou that art highly favored, the Lord is with thee: blessed art thou among women! Mary was troubled at his saying, and wondered what the meaning of it could be, but the angel said unto her, Fear not, Mary; for thou hast found favor with God. Then he told her how she should bear a son, whom she was to call Jesus, because he would save his people from their sins. He shall be great; and shall be called the Son of the Highest; and the Lord God shall give unto him the throne of his father David: and he shall reign over the house of Jacob forever; and of his kingdom there shall be no end. Mary wondered, but did not doubt like Zacharias. In deep humility she made answer, Behold the handmaid of the Lord; be it unto me according to thy word. Now Elizabeth, the wife of Zacharias, and Mary were cousins and the angel had told Mary that Elizabeth was to have a son; so Mary went to visit her and rejoice with her.

The great honor conferred upon Mary must have been revealed to Elizabeth, for when she entered her

THE ANGEL APPEARS TO ELIZABETH

house she said to her, Blessed art thou among women. But Mary, giving all the glory to God, burst forth into a hymn of praise, beginning, My soul doth magnify the Lord, and my spirit hath rejoiced in God my Saviour. Mary stayed with her cousin three months, and then returned home.

When Elizabeth's son was born, there was great joy in their house because of his birth. On the eighth day the child was circumcised, and the friends and relations wished to call him Zacharias, but his mother said, Not so, but he shall be called John. And they made signs to his father how he would have him called; and he asked for a writing-table, and wrote, His name is John.

And immediately the tongue of Zacharias was loosed, and he praised God. The people marvelled to see this, and asked one another, What manner of child shall this be?

At this time a decree was issued by the Roman Emperor that the Jews should be taxed. This caused much disturbance throughout the country, as those Jews scattered up and down had to find their way to their native city, there to answer to their names, and give an account of their possessions. Thus Joseph and Mary, being of the lineage of David, had to journey from Nazareth south to the city of David called Bethlehem. Here, shortly after their arrival, the holy child Jesus was born. Owing to the crowded state of the city there was no room for them in the inn, so the Lord Jesus found his first resting-place in a manger.

In the neighborhood of Bethlehem some shepherds were watching their flocks by night, probably owing

THE BIRTH OF JESUS

to the disturbed state of the country. Perhaps in the stillness of the night they were talking of the coming of the Messiah, when lo, a shining one appeared unto them, who said, Fear not, for behold, I bring you good tidings of great joy which shall be to all people. For unto you is born this day in the city of David a Saviour, which is Christ the Lord. And this shall be a sign unto you: Ye shall find the babe wrapped in swaddling-clothes, lying in a manger. When the angel finished speaking, there appeared a great company of the heavenly host, praising God, and this was their song: Glory to God in the highest, and on earth peace, good-will towards men. Then they returned to heaven, and when the shepherds had recovered from their amazement, they rose up and proceeded to Bethlehem, where they found Mary and the child, as the angel had said. They told Mary all they had seen, but she kept silence, and thought over all these things in her heart. Then the shepherds returned, glorifying and praising God.

When the holy child was eight days old he was circumcised, and received the name JESUS. After forty days had passed he was taken to the temple to be presented to the Lord, and also that Joseph might offer sacrifice according to the law of Moses.

While in the temple an aged man, called Simeon, seeing the holy child, through faith recognized him to be the Saviour, and taking him in his arms he uttered those beautiful words, Lord, now lettest thou thy servant depart in peace according to thy word: for mine eyes have seen thy salvation. And there was in the temple at the same time a prophetess

THE ANGELS APPEARING TO THE SHEPHERDS

called Anna, who also waited for the coming of the Saviour, and seeing him now she gave thanks to the Lord.

We can imagine how all these wonderful events would be talked over quietly among the people for fear of Herod, who was noted for his cowardice and cruelty. But in spite of all precautions the knowledge of the Saviour's birth came to him, and in a strange manner.

Far away in an eastern land, learned men had been studying the heavens. It was generally believed over all the then known world that a great deliverer was to be born unto the Jews, and his coming was to be indicated by a new star. These wise men having discovered a new star, followed its course, travelling by night, until they came to the land of Palestine. It was quite natural they should at once proceed to Jerusalem, the capital, and there expect to find this prince in one of its palaces. But to all their inquiries no one could give a satisfactory answer. Herod was troubled when he heard of the inquiries of these wise men, for he, like many others, believed that a prince and a ruler would come, and thus he would lose his kingdom. So he inquired of the chief priests where Christ should be born. They said in Bethlehem. He then desired the wise men, when they had found the child, to bring him word, that he might go and worship likewise. In this request he showed his treachery, for not worship but murder was the desire of Herod's heart.

The wise men then left Jerusalem, and seeing the star once more, they followed it until it stood over the

THE WISE MEN ADORING THE INFANT JESUS

place where the young child lay. Then they worshipped the Saviour, and laid at his feet the costly presents they had brought, which showed their love, obedience, and worship.

God having warned them in a dream not to return to Herod, they went to their own country by another way. And when Herod saw that the wise men did not return, he was very angry, and sent soldiers to Bethlehem to kill all the children of two years old and under.

But the Lord appeared to Joseph in a dream, and commanded him to take the young child and his mother, and flee into Egypt. And Joseph and Mary, with the young child, departed by night for the land of Egypt, where they remained until the danger was over.

After the death of Herod they returned to their home in the city of Nazareth. The country round about Nazareth is very beautiful, but what interests us most is not the beauty of the country so much as the thought that here the boyhood of Jesus was spent. We wonder how that boyhood was passed; what he said, and felt, especially about the world he had come to save. These questions cannot be answered. For twelve years the life of Jesus is wrapped in unbroken silence. We only know that he grew, and waxed strong in spirit, filled with wisdom, and the grace of God was upon him.

When Jesus was about twelve years old Joseph and Mary took him to Jerusalem to the feast of the Passover. This was a long journey from Nazareth, but it happened at a good season of the year, after the summer's heat and before the winter's rain be-

THE FLIGHT INTO EGYPT

gan to fall. When the feast was over, Joseph and Mary set out on their return journey, but Jesus tarried in Jerusalem, and Joseph and Mary were some distance from Jerusalem before Jesus was missed. Not finding him among their kinsfolk and friends, they returned to Jerusalem, and after three days they found him in the temple among the teachers of the law, both hearing and asking them questions. And when they saw him they were amazed, and his mother said, Son, why hast thou thus dealt with us? Behold, thy father and I have sought thee sorrowing. Jesus answered, How is it that ye sought me? Wist ye not that I must be about my Father's business? He would have his mother know that implicit obedience to his heavenly Father was the first rule of his life. Still, although the Son of God, he yielded to them the true obedience of a son, and returned with them to Nazareth, where, we doubt not, he labored with Joseph at the carpenter's bench for his own support and that of the family.

For the next eighteen years there is silence respecting the life of Jesus. We only know that he grew in wisdom and stature, and in favor with God and man.

While this quiet life at Nazareth was going on, John, the son of Zacharias and Elizabeth, was being prepared by the Holy Spirit for the great work he had to do. We are told that he was in the desert till the day of his showing unto Israel, that he was clothed with a garment of camel's hair, and with a leather girdle about his waist, and that his food consisted of locusts and wild honey.

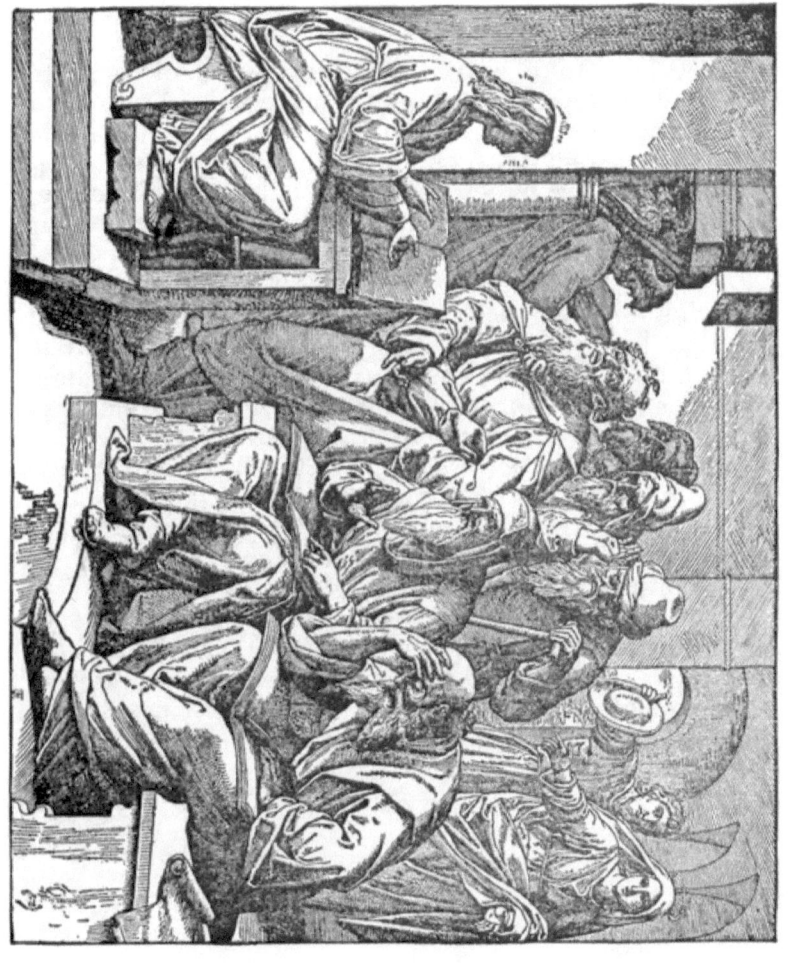
JESUS DISPUTING WITH THE DOCTORS.

When John was about thirty years of age the word of God came unto him in the wilderness; so in obedience to the command he went about all the country round Jordan, preaching the gospel of repentance, denouncing the evil habits of the people, and baptizing such as repented and confessed their sins. Hence he was called John the Baptist.

And when the people mused in their hearts whether John were the Christ or not, he told them that he indeed baptized them with water, but one mightier than he was coming, the latchet of whose shoe he was not worthy to unloose; he would baptize them with the Holy Ghost and with fire.

Then cometh Jesus from Galilee to Jordan unto John to be baptized. But John refused, saying that he had need to be baptized by him. But Jesus answered, Suffer it to be so; for thus it becometh us to fulfil all righteousness.

John then baptized Jesus, and as he came out of the water the heavens were opened, and he saw the Spirit of God descending like a dove, and lighting upon him; while a voice was heard, saying, This is my beloved Son, in whom I am well pleased.

JOHN PREACHING IN THE WILDERNESS

CHAPTER II

JESUS TEMPTED OF THE DEVIL—JESUS BEGINS HIS PUBLIC MINISTRY—THE BAPTIST SLAIN BY HEROD—HIS FIRST TWO DISCIPLES—HIS FIRST MIRACLE AT CANA—HE CASTS THE BUYERS AND SELLERS OUT OF THE TEMPLE—JESUS AND NICODEMUS—HE DISCOURSES TO A SAMARITAN WOMAN.

JESUS did not remain with John the Baptist, for the Spirit led him away into the wilderness, where he tarried forty days and forty nights, enduring the pangs of hunger and the assaults of the Evil One. A mystery we are unable to penetrate overshadows these forty days, but we know that there he suffered the first pangs of that grief with which he was wounded for our transgressions and bruised for our iniquities. He was tempted on all points like as we are, in order that when we draw near to him we may feel that there is no barrier between him and us, for in that he suffered being tempted he is able to succor them that are tempted.

While Jesus was in the wilderness the preaching and baptizing of John the Baptist attracted the attention of the Sanhedrim, or great council of the nation. It was their duty to inquire into any new religious rite, and investigate the authority and doctrine of any new preacher; therefore they sent some of their members to question John. They asked him if he were the Christ? or Elias? or that

THE TEMPTATION OF JESUS

prophet? To all these questions he answered, No. Then they said to him, Who art thou? What sayest thou of thyself? John answered, I am the voice of one crying in the wilderness, Make straight the way of the Lord, as said the prophet Isaiah. Evidently not understanding this answer, they inquired by what authority he baptized. He answered, I baptize with water, but there standeth one among you, whom ye know not; he it is who, coming after me, is preferred before me, whose shoe latchet I am not worthy to unloose. John after this became a marked man, and his enemies went so far as to say, He hath a devil.

After Jesus had returned from being tempted in the wilderness he went to the banks of the Jordan, where John was still preaching and baptizing. On observing Jesus approach, John exclaimed, Behold the Lamb of God, that taketh away the sin of the world. There were two of the Baptist's apostles with him when he uttered these words, and they immediately followed Jesus. One of them was Andrew; the other, whose name is not given, is generally supposed to be the apostle John. When Jesus saw them following, he turned and asked what they sought. They said, Master, where dwellest thou? Jesus said, Come and see; and they abode with him that day.

These men were fishermen, and this is the first beginning of the Christian Church.

The next day Andrew brought his brother Simon to Jesus, telling him he had found the Messiah. When Jesus saw Simon, he said to him, Thou art Simon, the son of Jona; thou shalt be called

JESUS CALLING HIS DISCIPLES.

Cephas, which is by interpretation a stone. Jesus, who could read the hearts of all men, saw in Peter a confident boldness, which when purified by the Holy Spirit would be serviceable to his cause. Hence the name he bestowed, Peter, a stone, or rock, meaning firmness, boldness, strength.

The next day Jesus called to him another disciple named Philip, probably a friend of Andrew and Peter. To him Jesus said, Follow me. He was willing to do so, but went first to his friend Nathanael, to whom he imparted the glad news of his finding in Jesus of Nazareth the Messiah. Nathanael belonged to the village of Cana, situated a few miles from Nazareth. He doubtingly asked Philip, Can any good thing come out of Nazareth? Philip answered, Come and see. When Jesus saw Nathanael coming, he said of him, Behold an Israelite indeed, in whom is no guile. Nathanael asked, Whence knowest thou me? Jesus replied, Before that Philip called thee, when thou wast under the fig-tree, I saw thee.

Then Nathanael believed, and said, Rabbi, thou art the Son of God. Nathanael is generally supposed to be the same apostle who bore the name of Bartholomew.

With these five followers, all natives of Galilee, began the public life of Jesus.

Some time after this John was cast into prison by Herod, because he had reproved him, and told him it was not lawful for him to have his brother's wife. For this Herod would have him put to death, but he feared the people, because they counted John a prophet. But Herodias, Herod's wife and companion in sin, hated John because of his reproof, and resolved that he should die.

She found a convenient time on Herod's birthday. Herod had adopted the celebration of birthdays from the Romans, and accordingly he gave a great supper, and invited his lords and his chief captains to it. And Salome, the daughter of Herodias by her former husband, appeared before the company and danced. She so pleased Herod and them that sat with him, that he swore unto her, Whatsoever thou shalt ask of me, I will give it thee, unto the half of my kingdom. And the young girl went to her mother, who told her to ask for the head of John the Baptist. And she returned and said to the king, Give me here John Baptist's head in a charger. And the king was sorry; nevertheless for his oath's sake, he commanded it to be given her. And John was beheaded in prison, and his head given to the damsel, and she took it to her mother.

We next find our Lord at Cana of Galilee, where a marriage was being celebrated. Mary, the mother of Jesus, was there, and he and his disciples were invited. The mother of Jesus seems to have taken some active part in the management of the feast, for on discovering that they wanted wine, she turned to Jesus and said, They have no wine. Jesus said, Woman, what have I to do with thee? Mine hour is not yet come. Then Mary said to the attendants, Whatsoever he sayeth to you, do it. Seeing six water-pots standing by, he told the servants to fill them with water to the brim, and then to draw forth. This they did, and bore it to the governor of the feast. Not being aware of the miracle, he tasted the wine, and called to the bridegroom, Every man at the beginning doth set forth good wine, but thou hast kept the good wine until now.

After this Jesus went with his mother and disciples to Capernaum, a city on the Sea of Galilee, and there remained a few days until the time for going up to Jerusalem to keep the feast of the Passover.

This was Jesus' first visit to Jerusalem since his baptism. On going into the temple he found three men selling oxen, sheep and doves; also the changers of money. And when he had made a scourge of small cords, he drove them out of the temple with it, saying, Take these things hence: make not my Father's house an house of merchandise.

And when the Jews asked him for a sign that he had a right to do this, he replied, Destroy this temple, and in three days I will raise it up. Then said the Jews, Forty and six years was this temple in building, and wilt thou rear it up in three days? Jesus spake of the temple of his body, but they did not understand. Neither did his disciples at that time, but after the resurrection they remembered his words.

During the Passover week Jesus wrought many miracles, and many believed on him because of the miracles, but their faith was weak.

Among these was a man named Nicodemus, one of the Pharisees, and a ruler of the Jews. He came to Jesus by night, being unwilling probably to commit himself publicly to the new doctrine. He admitted to Jesus that he knew he was a teacher come from God from the miracles which he did. Jesus expounded to him the nature of the new birth, saying to him, Except a man be born of water and of

CHANGING THE WATER INTO WINE

the spirit, he cannot enter into the kingdom of God. When Nicodemus asked, How can these things be? Jesus said, As Moses lifted up the serpent in the wilderness, even so must the Son of Man be lifted up: that whosoever believeth in him should not perish, but have eternal life. For God so loved the world, that he gave his only-begotten Son, that whosoever believeth in him should not perish, but have everlasting life.

After this Jesus left Jerusalem, and came into Judea, but the jealousy of the Pharisees compelled him to depart again into Galilee. Between Judea and Galilee lay the country of Samaria, and Jesus must needs go through that country, although the hostility of the Samaritans to the Jews was well known. When he came near to a city called Sychar, being wearied with his journey, he sat down to rest, by a well, called Jacob's Well, while his disciples went into the town to buy bread. As he sat there a Samaritan woman came out to draw water. Jesus said to her, Give me to drink. She expressed her surprise at a Jew asking a favor from a Samaritan. But Jesus said, If thou knewest the gift of God, and who it is that saith to thee, Give me to drink, thou wouldst have asked of him, and he would have given thee living water. The woman understood not this saying about living water, but Jesus said to her, Whosoever drinketh of this water shall thirst again: but whosoever drinketh of the water that I shall give him shall never thirst; for it shall be a well of water springing up into everlasting life. Then he revealed to her that he knew all her past life; and the woman said, Sir, I believe that thou art a prophet. Jesus

DRIVING THE SELLERS FROM THE TEMPLE

went on to speak unto her of the spiritual nature of worship, teaching her the great truth that God is a Spirit, and they that worship him must do so in spirit and truth. When the woman had declared that she knew about the promised Messiah, Jesus said to her, I that speak unto thee am he.

When the disciples returned they were astonished to find Jesus engaged in talking with a Samaritan woman, but they asked him no questions. The woman then left her water-pot, and called on her friends and neighbors to come and see a man who had told her all things that ever she did, saying, Is not this the Christ? And they followed her.

In the meantime the disciples were urging Jesus to eat, saying, Master, eat. But he answered, I have meat to eat that ye know not of. The disciples said one to another, Hath any man brought him aught to eat? Jesus said, My meat is to do the will of him that sent me, and to finish his work.

Many of the Samaritans believed on him for the saying of the woman, and besought him that he would tarry with them. Our Lord yielded to their request, and remained two days. And many more believed because of his own word; and said unto the woman, Now we believe, not because of thy saying; for we have heard him ourselves, and know this is indeed the Christ, the Saviour of the world.

JESUS AND THE WOMAN OF SAMARIA.

CHAPTER III

JESUS HEALS THE NOBLEMAN'S SON—HE TEACHES IN THE SYNAGOGUE AT NAZARETH—THE MIRACLE OF THE FISHES—HE TEACHES IN THE SYNAGOGUE AT CAPERNAUM—AN UNCLEAN SPIRIT CAST OUT—PETER'S WIFE'S MOTHER HEALED—OTHER MIRACLES OF HEALING—MATTHEW CALLED TO BE AN APOSTLE.

OUR Lord now went into Galilee, where he was well received by the people. They had been at the Passover in Jerusalem, and had seen his wonderful works there.

Jesus came again into Cana, where he had performed his first miracle by turning water into wine, and it was now to be the scene of his second.

A certain nobleman, whose son was sick at Capernaum, hearing that Jesus had come to Galilee, went unto him, and requested him to come down and heal his son, for he was at the point of death. But Jesus said to him, Except ye see signs and wonders, ye will not believe. The nobleman, not disheartened by this reply, said, Sir, come down ere my child die. Then Jesus said, Go thy way, thy son liveth. The nobleman believed the word that Jesus had spoken, and went his way.

Next day, as he was going down to Capernaum, his servants met him, and said, Thy son liveth. On inquiring at what hour the child began to mend, he found it to be the same at which Jesus said, Thy son liveth. And the nobleman and his whole house believed in Jesus.

And Jesus came to Nazareth, the city of his childhood, and as his custom was, went into the synagogue on the Sabbath day, and stood up to read. And they handed to him the Book of Isaiah, and Jesus opened the book and read, The Spirit of the Lord is upon me, because he hath anointed me to preach the gospel to the poor; he hath sent me to heal the broken-hearted, to preach deliverance to the captives, and recovering of sight to the blind, to set at liberty them that are bruised, to preach the acceptable year of the Lord.

He then closed the book, and returning it to the minister, sat down. All eyes were now fastened upon Jesus, and he said unto them, This day is this scripture fulfilled in your ears. And they wondered at the gracious words which proceeded out of his mouth, and said one to another, Is not this Joseph's son? But Jesus knew their thoughts, and said, Ye will surely say unto me this proverb, Physician, heal thyself; whatsoever we have heard done in Capernaum, do also here in thy country. But verily, I say unto you, no prophet is accepted in his own country. He then reminded them that although there were many widows in Israel when it rained not for three years and six months, yet Elijah went to none of them save unto the widow of Sarepta, a city of Sidon. And many lepers were in Israel in the days of Elisha, but none were cleansed but Naaman the Syrian. They understood his meaning—namely, that if they rejected him, he would turn to the Gentiles. And they were filled with wrath, and rushing out of the synagogue they thrust Jesus out of the city, and led him to the brow of the hill on which the city was built, that they might cast him down headlong. But Jesus' hour was not yet come, and passing through the midst of them he went his way.

Leaving Nazareth, Jesus journeyed towards Capernaum, a city of Galilee, where he taught on the Sabbath days. And the people were astonished at his doctrine, for his word was with power, and they brought unto him them that were sick with divers diseases, and he laid his hands on them and healed them.

While he stood by the shore of the lake, the people pressed upon him to hear the word of God, and seeing two ships lying at the water's edge, Jesus requested Simon to thrust out a little from the land. And he sat down and taught the people out of the ship.

When he had done speaking, Jesus told Peter to launch out into the deep, and let down his nets for a draught. Peter obeyed, but said they had toiled all night and had caught nothing. On drawing up the net, it was so full they beckoned unto their partners in the other ship to come and help. And both the ships were filled, so that they began to sink. When Peter saw this miracle, he fell down at the feet of Jesus, saying, Depart from me, for I am a sinful man, O Lord! Jesus said unto him, Fear not; from henceforth thou shalt catch men. When they had brought their ships to land, they left all and followed Jesus. And when he had gone a little further Jesus saw James and John, the sons of Zebedee, mending

THE MIRACULOUS DRAUGHT OF FISHES.

their nets, and straightway he called them; and they left their father Zebedee in the ship with the hired servants, and went after him.

The next Sabbath day Jesus again repaired to the synagogue, and taught the people; and they were astonished at his doctrine, for he taught them as one that had authority, and not as the scribes.

While he was speaking, there was in the synagogue a man with an unclean spirit, and he cried out, Let us alone; what have we to do with thee, thou Jesus of Nazareth? art thou come to destroy us? I know thee, who thou art, the holy one of God. And Jesus rebuked the unclean spirit, and commanded it to come out of the man. And when it had torn him, it came out of him, crying with a loud voice.

This was the first miracle of this kind Jesus had wrought. The people were filled with amazement, and the fame of Jesus spread abroad throughout all the region round about Galilee.

After the miracle Jesus retired to Simon Peter's house. There he found Peter's mother-in-law lying sick of a fever. He went to her, and taking her by the hand, lifted her up; and immediately the fever left her, and she arose and ministered unto them.

And at even they brought unto him they that were sick, and them that were possessed with devils, and he had compassion on them and healed them.

In the morning he rose early, a great while before day, and seeking out a solitary place, held communion with his Father in heaven. But Simon, and they that were with him, followed him, and said, All men seek thee. And he said unto them, Let us go into the next town, that I may preach there also; for therefor came I forth. And he preached in their synagogues throughout all Galilee, and cast out devils.

And there came a man to him afflicted with the loathsome and incurable disease of leprosy, and kneeling down, he said, Lord, if thou wilt, thou canst make me clean. Jesus, looking at him with eyes full of pity, put forth his hand, and touching him, said, I will; be thou clean. And his leprosy departed from him. And Jesus charged him to tell no man, but go to the priest, and offer for his cleansing the things commanded by Moses. But the man noised abroad his cure, so that Jesus could no longer enter the city openly, but withdrew to desert places.

After some days Jesus returned again to Capernaum, and as soon as it was known great crowds followed, insomuch that there was no room in the house where he was to receive them; and he preached the word unto them. While he was speaking, four men carrying a bed, in which lay a paralytic man, tried to reach Jesus, but they could not come nigh unto him for the crowd. So they uncovered the roof and let down the bed whereon lay the paralytic man. When Jesus saw their faith, he said unto the sick man, Son, thy sins be forgiven thee. But the scribes who sat there reasoned in their hearts, Why doth this man thus speak blasphemies? Who can forgive sins but God? Jesus, answering their unspoken thoughts, asked them whether it was easier to say, Thy sins be forgiven thee, or Arise, and take up thy bed, and walk? And to show that he had all power he turned to the palsied man, and said, Arise, and take up thy bed, and go thy way into thine house. And immediately he arose, took up the bed, and went forth before them all. And they were all amazed, and glorified God.

After this Jesus walked again by the shore of the lake, and he passed by a man sitting at the "receipt of custom," that is, collecting the Roman taxes from the people. These tax collectors were called Publicans, and were hated by the people. From one of this class our Lord now chose his next disciple, saying to Levi, the tax collector, Follow me. And he arose and followed him. He was afterwards known by the name of Matthew, and to his pen we owe the first of the Gospels. And Jesus went to Matthew's house, and sat down to meat with him and many other Publicans. And the Pharisees were surprised at Jesus eating and drinking with Publicans and sinners. But when he heard it, he said, They that are whole have no need of the physician, but they that are sick; I came not to call the righteous, but sinners to repentance.

CURING THE PARALYTIC

CHAPTER IV

THE RAISING OF JAIRUS' DAUGHTER—THE HEALING OF THE WOMAN WHO TOUCHED THE HEM OF JESUS' GARMENT, OF TWO BLIND MEN, OF A DUMB MAN, OF THE MAN AT THE POOL OF BETHESDA—THE PHARISEES REBUKED—THE HEALING OF THE MAN WITH THE WITHERED HAND—THE TWELVE APOSTLES CHOSEN—THE SERMON ON THE MOUNT—THE HEALING OF THE CENTURION'S SERVANT—THE SON OF A WIDOW AT NAIN RAISED FROM THE DEAD—A WOMAN WASHES JESUS' FEET WITH HER TEARS—HE CASTS OUT A DEVIL.

AT this time one of the rulers of the synagogue, named Jairus, came to Jesus, beseeching him to come and raise his daughter, who lay dying. She was his only daughter, aged twelve years. Such was the faith of the ruler that he thought if Jesus would but lay his hand upon her she would live. Jesus went with him, and a large crowd followed after.

And as he went, a woman came behind him and touched the hem of his garment. She had an incurable disease, and she said to herself, If I may but touch his garment, I shall be whole. Jesus turned, and seeing the woman, said unto her, Daughter, thy faith hath made thee whole. And she was whole from that hour.

On reaching the house of the ruler he found it full of people, weeping and lamenting over the child. Putting them all out save the father and

THE RAISING OF JAIRUS' DAUGHTER

mother, and Peter, James, and John, Jesus took the child by the hand, and said to her, Maid, arise; and her spirit came again, and she straightway arose. And Jesus commanded them to give her meat. The parents were astonished at this miracle, and although they were charged to tell no man, the fame of it went through all the land.

When Jesus departed thence two blind men followed him, crying, Thou Son of David, have mercy upon us. Jesus said to them, Believe ye that I am able to do this? And they said, Yea, Lord. Jesus then touched their eyes and they immediately received their sight. And he charged them that they should tell no man; but they immediately departed, and spread it abroad in all the country.

And a dumb man was brought to him who had a devil. Jesus cast out the evil spirit, and the dumb man spake.

The people were astonished at these wonderful cures, and said that such things had never been seen in Israel before; but the Pharisees said, He casteth out devils through the prince of the devils. But Jesus went through all the towns and villages, preaching in the synagogues, and healing all kinds of sickness.

We next find our Lord in Jerusalem. There was a pool near by the sheep gate of the city, which was supposed to possess the power of healing diseases. It was called the pool of Bethesda, which means "House of Mercy." Thither resorted many impotent folk—the blind, the lame, and paralytics. At a certain season an angel came down and troubled the water, and whoever was first dipped after the troubling of the water was cured of his disease. One man, who had been lame for thirty-eight years, had lain a long time at the side of the pool, but having no friends to help him, others more nimble than himself reached the water first, and received the benefit. Jesus passing by saw this poor man, and having pity on him, he put the question to him, Wilt thou be made whole? The man explained his situation to our Lord, and he said to him, Rise, take up thy bed, and walk. And immediately he was made whole, and took up his bed and walked. This happened on the Sabbath day; and the Jews immediately said to the man, It is not lawful for thee to carry thy bed on the Sabbath day. The man answered that he who had cured him commanded him to take up his bed and carry it; but that he did not know who the man was. Afterwards Jesus found the man in the temple, and bade him go and sin no more, lest a worse fate should befall him.

He then went and told the Jews that it was Jesus who had cured him, and they sought to kill him, because he had healed on the Sabbath day. Jesus answered them, My Father worketh hitherto, and I work. This answer made them still more angry, for Jesus had said that God was his Father, and thus made himself equal with God. Jesus then answered them, Verily, verily, I say unto you, the Son can do nothing of himself, but what he seeth the Father do: for what things soever he doeth, these also doeth the Son likewise. For the Father loveth the Son, and showeth him all things that himself doeth: and he will show him greater works than these, that ye may marvel. He went to warn them that the Father had committed all judgment to him, the Son, and that the hour was coming when all men would honor the Son even as they honored the Father. The Father, he told them, had already borne witness to him, the Son; but as they had not the word of the Father abiding in them, they did not believe on him whom the Father had sent. He also declared unto them that if they had believed their great prophet Moses, they would also have believed on him, for Moses wrote of him.

Again it is the Sabbath day, and Jesus walked through the fields with his disciples; and the disciples being hungry, as they walked plucked the ears of corn and rubbed them between the palms of their hands and did eat.

The Pharisees, ever ready to find fault, asked the disciples why they did that which was unlawful to do on the Sabbath day. But Jesus reminded them that when King David was hungry, he went into the house of God and did eat the shewbread, which no one should eat save the priests only, and gave also to them who were with him. He concluded by telling them that the Son of man was Lord also of the Sabbath.

On another Sabbath day Jesus entered the synagogue and taught; and there was there a man whose right hand was withered. And the Pharisees watched whether he would heal on the Sabbath day, that they might find an accusation against him. Jesus knew their thoughts, and commanded the man to stand up in the midst. Then said Jesus to the Pharisees, Is it lawful on the Sabbath days to do good, or to do evil? to save life, or to destroy it? And looking round on them all, he ordered the man to stretch forth his hand; and when he did so, it was restored whole as the other. Then the Pharisees became mad with rage, and took counsel together how they might kill Jesus; but his hour was not yet come, so he removed himself from that place, and returned once more to Galilee.

On reaching Galilee he called together his disciples, and chose out from among them twelve apostles, or messengers, as the word means. They were to go out to teach; and he imparted to them miraculous powers. Their names were Peter and Andrew, James and John, Philip and Bartholomew, Matthew and Thomas, James, the son of Alphæus, Judas, the brother of James, Simon Zelotes, and Judas Iscariot.

Seeing the multitudes which followed him, Jesus ascended a mountain, and there delivered to his disciples the discourse called the Sermon on the Mount, of which the following is a part, commonly called the Beatitudes:

"Blessed are the poor in spirit: for theirs is the kingdom of heaven. Blessed are they that mourn: for they shall be comforted. Blessed are the meek: for they shall inherit the earth. Blessed are they which do hunger and thirst after righteousness: for they shall be filled. Blessed are the merciful: for they shall obtain mercy. Blessed are the pure in heart: for they shall see God. Blessed are the peacemakers: for they shall be called the children of God. Blessed are they which are persecuted for righteousness' sake: for theirs is the kingdom of heaven.

Blessed are ye, when men shall revile you, and persecute you, and shall say all manner of evil against you falsely, for my sake. Rejoice, and be exceeding glad; for great is your reward in heaven; for so persecuted they the prophets which were before you."

In this sermon Jesus taught his disciples, among other things, the spiritual nature of his kingdom; how to keep the commandments; how to pray and fast; warned them against avarice; reproved rash judgments; and exhorted them to enter in at the strait gate. He concluded the discourse by likening those who heard his sayings, and did them, to a wise man who built his house upon a rock, and when the storm came his house fell not, being founded on a rock. Those, on the other hand, who heard his sayings, and did them not, he likened to a foolish man who built his house upon the sand, and when the storm came his house fell, and great was the fall thereof. After finishing his discourse Jesus proceeded to Capernaum.

A Roman centurion—that is, a captain of a hundred soldiers—stationed in that city, had a servant whom he loved lying sick and ready to die. When he heard of Jesus he sent to the elders of the city, begging them to intercede with him that he might heal his servant. This they willingly did, for the centurion had built a synagogue and loved the Jews. The elders told Jesus this, and he went with them. But the centurion when he heard this went to meet Jesus and said, Lord, I am not worthy that thou shouldest come under my roof, but speak the word only, and my servant shall be healed. When Jesus

THE SERMON ON THE MOUNT.

heard this he marvelled, and turning to his followers, said, I have not found so great faith, no, not in Israel. He then told the centurion to go his way, and it would be to him as he had believed. The servant was made whole that same hour.

The next day Jesus went into a city called Nain. As he approached the gate, he met the people carrying a young man to his grave; and he was the only son of his mother, and she was a widow. When Jesus saw her he was full of compassion, and said to her, Weep not. And he touched the bier, and said, Young man, I say unto thee, Arise. And the young man arose, and began to speak, and Jesus delivered him to his mother. And the people were afraid, but gave the glory to God, and said that a great prophet had risen up among them, and that God had visited his people.

And one of the Pharisees, called Simon, invited Jesus to dine at his house. And he went in and sat down to meat. As he reclined at the table, a woman of the city, who was a sinner, when she knew that Jesus was there, came in, bringing with her an alabaster box of ointment, and she stood behind Jesus weeping, and began to wash his feet with her tears, wiping them with the hairs of her head, kissing them, and anointing them with the ointment. The Pharisee saw this, and thought to himself that if Jesus was really a great prophet, he would have known what kind of woman this was who touched him, and would have sent her away. Jesus knowing his thoughts, said to him, Simon, I have somewhat to say unto thee. And Simon said, Master, say on. And Jesus said, There was a certain creditor which

FORGIVENESS AND LOVE.

had two debtors; the one owed five hundred pence, and the other fifty. And when they had nothing to pay, he frankly forgave them both. Tell me therefore which of them will love him most? Simon answered, I suppose the one to whom he forgave most. Jesus said he had rightly judged, and turning to the woman, added, Simon, seest thou this woman? I entered into thine house, thou gavest me no water for my feet; but she hath washed my feet with tears, and wiped them with the hairs of her head. Thou gavest me no kiss; but this woman since I came in hath not ceased to kiss my feet. My head with oil thou didst anoint; but this woman hath anointed my feet with ointment. Wherefore I say unto thee, her sins, which are many, are forgiven; for she loved much: but to whom little is forgiven, the same loveth little. Then he said to the woman, Thy sins are forgiven thee. And they that sat at the table said, Who is this that forgiveth sins also?

Jesus then began another tour through Galilee with his disciples, and he went into every city and village, showing the glad tidings of the kingdom of God. And they brought to him a man possessed with a devil, blind and dumb. Jesus cast out the devil, and the man could see and also speak. But the Pharisees said, He casteth out devils through Beelzebub, the prince of the devils. And Jesus reasoned with them, showing them that as a city divided against itself could not stand, so if Satan cast out Satan, then he would be fighting against himself, and how could his kingdom stand? He warned them that for all manner of sin men would be forgiven, except for blasphemy against the Holy Ghost, which would not be forgiven.

A woman in the crowd, hearing the wise and holy words which fell from the lips of Jesus, called out that the mother of one so good was blessed indeed; but Jesus answered that they were more blessed who hearing his word obeyed it. Mary his mother must have been in the vicinity, for a message was given to Jesus that his mother and brethren wished to speak with him. But he asked who was his mother, and who were his brethren. Stretching forth his hand, he said, Behold my mother and my brethren! For whosoever shall do the will of my Father which is in heaven, the same is my brother, and sister, and mother.

On this occasion our Lord received another invitation from a Pharisee to dine with him. He went in, and sat down to meat. The Pharisee was surprised that he washed not his hands before dinner; but Jesus denounced the Pharisees for their strictness as regarded outward observances, while their hearts were full of all wickedness. At the same time Jesus warned his disciples against hypocrisy, telling them there was nothing hidden but what would be made known; also that they were not to be afraid of what man could do to them, for man could kill only the body, while God could kill the soul. He reminded them that five sparrows were sold for two farthings, and not one of them could fall to the ground without his Father's knowledge; that the very hairs of their heads were numbered: they were, therefore, not to be afraid, for they were of more value than many sparrows.

CHAPTER V

THE PARABLE OF THE RICH MAN, OF THE SOWER, OF THE TARES, OF THE MUSTARD SEED, OF THE HIDDEN TREASURE, OF THE NET—JESUS STILLS THE WAVES—HE HEALS A DEMONIAC—SENDS OUT THE DISCIPLES TWO AND TWO—THE FEEDING OF THE FIVE THOUSAND—HE AGAIN STILLS THE WAVES—THE HEALING OF THE SYRO-PHŒ-NICIAN WOMAN'S DAUGHTER.

ONE of the company who had been listening to the last discourse of Jesus asked him to be a judge between him and his brother, who was treating him unjustly, in that he would not divide the inheritance with him. Jesus said, Man, who made me a judge or a divider over you? And by way of warning all present against the sin of covetousness, he spoke the following parable:

The grounds of a certain rich man had brought forth so plentifully that his barns would not hold all his fruits. Wondering what he should do, he resolved to pull down his barns and build greater, and then say to himself, that as he had much goods stored away for many years, he might take his ease, eat, drink, and be merry. But God said to him, Thou fool, this night thy soul shall be required of thee, then whose shall those things be which thou hast provided?

Jesus then told his disciples to take no thought for themselves, what they should eat, nor what they should wear, calling to their remembrance how the birds neither sowed nor reaped, nor stored up into barns, and yet they were fed: and asking them to consider the lilies, how they grew, though they toiled not nor spun, and yet Solomon in all his glory was not arrayed like one of them. If God then cared for these things, how much more would he care for them! They were to seek the kingdom of God, and all needful things would be given unto them.

After this Jesus was at the seaside, and great multitudes followed him. He therefore went into one of the fishing-boats, and sitting down spoke unto them the parable of the sower, meaning thereby to show how the preached Word is received by the different classes of hearers. Some of the seed, he said, fell upon the hard, beaten path which ran along the edge of the field, and the birds came and picked it up. This represented the wayside hearers, the inattentive ones, who hear but do not heed. And some fell upon stony places, where there was a little earth. This grew quickly, and as quickly withered away, because there was not depth of soil to sustain growth. Those are they who hear the Word with joy, but having no root in themselves, when persecution ariseth they are offended. And some fell among thorns, and the thorns sprang up and choked the seed. These are the hearers who allow the cares, and riches, and pleasures of this life to choke the Word, and thus are unfruitful. But some of the seed fell upon good soil, and brought forth fruit thirty-fold, sixty-fold, and even a hundred-fold. This represents those who listen to the Word, and understand it and bring forth fruit unto life eternal.

And Jesus spake another parable unto them of a

man who sowed good seed in his field, but while his servants slept an enemy came and sowed tares. When the blade sprang up, then appeared the tares also. The servants asked if the seed was not good which had been sown. Yes, the master said, but an enemy hath done this. Wait until the harvest, when the reapers will separate the tares from the wheat; the former to be burned, and the latter to be stored in the barn. The field, Jesus explained, was the world; the sower of good seed, himself. The good seed are the children of God; the bad seed the children of the wicked one. The enemy who came by night and sowed bad seed is Satan; the harvest is the end of the world; and the reapers are the angels. At the judgment day the angels shall gather the wicked ones and cast them out into outer darkness; while the righteous shall shine forth as the sun in the kingdom of their Father.

Again Jesus likened the growth of the kingdom of God to a mustard seed, which is the smallest of all seeds, and yet when it is planted it grows so large that the birds can find shelter among its branches.

He also compared the kingdom of heaven to a treasure hid in a field; which, when a man finds, he hideth, and for joy goes and sells all that he hath, and buys that field. He also compared the kingdom of heaven to a merchant seeking goodly pearls, who when he finds one pearl of great price, sells all that he possesses, and buys it.

Jesus next compared the end of the world to a net cast into the sea, which gathered all sorts of fish. When it was full they drew it ashore, gathered the good into vessels, and cast the bad away. So would it be at the latter day. And a scribe, or teacher of the law, came to Jesus, and said to him, Master, I will follow thee whithersoever thou goest. This drew forth from Jesus the answer, so indicative of his poverty, The foxes have holes, and the birds of the air have nests; but the Son of Man hath not where to lay his head.

After Jesus had spoken these things, he entered into a boat along with his disciples, and sailed for the opposite shore of the lake of Galilee. Being weary with the labors of the day he fell asleep, and while he slept a sudden tempest arose, insomuch that the boat was covered with the waves. The disciples were afraid, and awoke him with the cry, Master, carest thou not that we perish? Then Jesus arose and rebuked the wind and waves, commanding them to be still; and immediately there was a great calm. Then turning to the disciples, he asked them, Why are ye so fearful? how is it that ye have no faith? And they were afraid, and wondered what sort of a man this was, that even the winds and the sea obeyed him.

When they reached the other side they were met by a demoniac, who dwelt among the tombs. So furious was this man that no one was able to bind him, not even with chains. But when he saw Jesus afar off, he ran and worshipped him, crying with a loud voice, What have I to do with thee, Jesus, thou Son of the Most High God? I adjure thee by God that thou torment me not. Jesus commanded the evil spirits to come out of the man, and when they besought him that he would not send them out of the country, he gave them leave to enter into a herd of swine close by. Immediately the herd of swine, in number about two thousand, ran down a steep place into the sea and perished. Then they that fed the swine fled to the city, and told what they had seen, and the inhabitants came out to meet Jesus; but when they saw the demoniac sitting at his feet, clothed and in his right mind, they were afraid, and begged Jesus that he would depart from their coasts. Jesus returned to the boat; and when the poor man who had been cured desired to follow him, he bade him go home to his friends and tell them what had taken place. So he departed, and began to publish what great things God had done for him. Jesus returned again to the other side, where the people gathered to meet him, and heard him gladly.

He now called his disciples together, and sent them out, two and two, to preach the Gospel, giving them power to work miracles. He also instructed them how to act under all circumstances, telling them they would be as sheep in the midst of wolves; but they were to be as wise as serpents and harmless as doves. He warned them that they would be persecuted, and taken before kings and governors for his sake; but they were not to be afraid: for whosoever confessed him before men, him would he confess before his Father in heaven.

How long the disciples were absent we do not know, but on their return they gathered themselves around Jesus, and told him all the things they had done, and what they had taught. And he said to them, Come ye yourselves apart into a desert place, and rest awhile. And they departed into a desert place by ship privately. But the people saw this, and ran round the end of the lake, and reached the landing-place first; so there was a great crowd awaiting Jesus when he reached the shore. And he had pity on them, and taught them, and healed their sick. The disciples then urged him to send the multitude away; but Jesus had compassion on them, for they were faint; and, turning to Philip, he asked, Whence shall we buy bread that these may eat? Jesus himself knew what he would do, but he asked this question to try the faith of Philip, who only thought of the large sum of money it would take to feed so many. Jesus asked the disciples how many loaves they had, and Andrew replied that there was a lad in the crowd who had five loaves and two small fishes. He commanded them to seat the people in companies of fifty upon the grass. He then took the loaves, and when he had given thanks he distributed to the disciples, and the disciples to the multitude; and in like manner with the fishes. And when they had enough, Jesus commanded that the fragments might be gathered up. And there were gathered twelve baskets full, the number that was fed being about five thousand.

Jesus, desiring to be alone, caused his disciples to enter their ship, and cross over to Bethsaida, at the same time sending the people away. He then retired to a mountain to pray. Night came on, and the disciples were yet far from land, for the wind was contrary; and when Jesus saw them toiling in rowing, he came unto them, walking on the water. But when they saw him they were afraid, thinking it was a spirit, and cried out. Jesus said, Be of good cheer, it is I; be not afraid. Peter answered and said, Lord, if it be thou, bid me come unto thee on the water. Jesus said, Come. Peter went over the side of the ship, and at first he walked safely, but when he saw the boisterousness of the wind he began to sink, crying, Lord, save me. Jesus stretched out his hand, and caught him, saying, O thou of little faith, wherefore didst thou doubt? Jesus then entered the ship, when the wind abated.

The next day the people flocked down to the shore expecting to find Jesus, but not seeing him, they took shipping, and crossed the lake. When they found him they said, Rabbi, when camest thou hither? Jesus did not satisfy their curiosity, but told them the reason why they had sought him out. He said, Ye seek me, not because ye saw the miracles, but because ye did eat of the loaves and were filled. Labor not for the meat which perisheth, but for that meat which endureth unto everlasting life, which the Son of Man shall give unto you: for him hath God the Father sealed. They then asked him how they would work the works of God. He answered them that the work of God was to believe on him whom God had sent. They then demanded of him a sign, saying that Moses fed their fathers with manna as a sign of his commission. Jesus answered that the bread which Moses gave their fathers was not the bread from heaven; but, he added, I am the bread of life: he that cometh to me shall never hunger; and he that believeth on me shall never thirst. They then began to murmur because he said he was the bread from heaven, when they knew he was the

FEEDING THE MULTITUDE

son of Joseph and Mary. But Jesus told them not to murmur among themselves; for he said, No man can come to me, except the Father, which hath sent me, draw him: and I will raise him up at the last day. Many of his disciples when they heard this discourse said, This is an hard saying : who can hear it? And they went back, and walked no more with him. Then he turned to the twelve, and said, Will ye also go away? This drew from Simon Peter the reply, Lord, to whom shall we go? Thou hast the words of eternal life. And we believe and are sure that thou art that Christ, the Son of the living God.

Then Jesus went thence and departed into the regions of Tyre and Sidon. And a Gentile woman, a Syro-Phœnician by nation, whose daughter had an unclean spirit, sought him that he would heal her. But Jesus answered her not a word; and the disciples requested that she might be sent away. Jesus then said unto her that he was only sent unto the lost sheep of the house of Israel. But she fell down and worshipped him, saying, Lord, help me. He replied, It is not meet to take the children's bread and to cast it to dogs. She was not discouraged by the reply, but answered, Truth, Lord; yet the dogs eat of the crumbs which fall from their master's table. Then he said, O woman, great is thy faith: be it unto thee even as thou wilt. And her daughter was made whole that very hour.

CHAPTER VI

MORE MIRACLES OF HEALING—THE PHARISEES AND SADDUCEES DEMAND A SIGN—THE TRANSFIGURATION—JESUS GOES UP TO JERUSALEM—THE PARABLE OF THE GOOD SAMARITAN—JESUS AT BETHANY—THE PARABLE OF THE PRODIGAL SON.

WE next find our Lord on the shore of the Sea of Galilee. There they brought to him one who was deaf and had an impediment in his speech, and they besought him to put his hand upon him. Jesus took him aside, and put his fingers in his ears, spat, and touched his tongue, then looking up to heaven he sighed, and uttered the word, "Ephphatha!" that is, "be opened!" and immediately the man could both hear and speak.

And great crowds came round Jesus, bringing with them the lame, the blind, the dumb, the maimed, and many others, and casting them down at Jesus' feet; and he healed them.

And Jesus had compassion on this multitude, as he had on a former occasion, and again fed them miraculously, the provision in this case being seven loaves and a few small fishes, while the fragments which remained filled seven baskets. Four thousand men at this time ate and were filled, beside women and children. And Jesus sent them away, while he and the disciples entered a ship, and came to Magdala.

Here the Pharisees and Sadducees came tempting

our Lord, and asking that he should show them a sign from heaven. He denounced them as hypocrites, telling them that they could discern the signs of fair and foul weather, but they could not discern the signs of the times. He also told them no sign should be given them except the sign of the prophet Jonah, meaning, that as Jonah was in the belly of the whale for three days, so would he be buried for three days in the earth.

Again Jesus entered a ship, and as they were crossing to the other side he warned his disciples against the evil example and teachings of the Pharisees, likening their influence to leaven spreading through flour. On landing at Bethsaida, a blind man was brought to Jesus that he might receive his sight. In this case, as in the former one of the deaf and dumb man, our Lord took him out of the town, and having anointed his eyes, touched them, and asked if he saw anything. The man replied that he saw men as trees walking. Then Jesus touched him again, and made him look up, and he saw everything clearly.

Jesus and his disciples now turned northwards in the direction of Cæsarea Philippi, and while on the way he began to teach them what things were about to befall him in Jerusalem: how that the Son of Man would be rejected of the elders and the chief priests, and be killed, and buried, and after three days he would rise again. He also taught them, that if any man wished to be his disciple, he must deny himself, and take up his cross, and follow him. For whosoever will save his life shall lose it; but whosoever shall lose his life for my sake and the gospel's, the same shall save it. For what shall it profit a man,

JESUS RESTORES SIGHT TO THE BLIND MAN.

if he shall gain the whole world, and lose his own soul? Or what shall a man give in exchange for his soul? After six days Jesus took with him Peter, and James, and John, and led them up into a high mountain to pray. And as he prayed, the fashion of his countenance was altered, and his raiment was white and glistering. And, behold, there talked with him two men, which were Moses and Elias: who appeared in glory, and spake of his decease which he should accomplish at Jerusalem. But Peter and they that were with him were heavy with sleep: and when they were awake, they saw his glory, and the two men that stood with him.

And Peter, not knowing what he said, cried out unto Jesus, Master, it is good for us to be here; and let us make three tabernacles, one for thee, and one for Moses, and one for Elias. And while he spoke a bright cloud overshadowed them, and a voice came out of the cloud, saying, This is my beloved Son; hear him. The disciples were sore afraid, and fell on their faces; but Jesus came and touched them, and bade them arise, and be not afraid. As they came down from the mountain, Jesus charged them that they should tell no man what they had seen until the Son of Man had risen from the dead.

When they joined the other disciples they found them surrounded by a great multitude, and being questioned by the scribes. Jesus asked them, Why question ye them? A man in the crowd answered that he had a son afflicted with a dumb spirit, which dashed him about, and caused him to foam and gnash with his teeth, and that he had asked the disciples to cure him, but they could not. Jesus upbraided his disciples with their want of faith, and commanded that the patient should be brought to him. Then, turning to the father, he said, If thou canst believe, all things are possible to him that believeth. Straightway the father cried out with tears, Lord, I believe; help thou mine unbelief. Jesus at once rebuked the spirit, and charged it to come out of the lad, which it did, leaving him as one dead. But he took him by the hand, and he arose. And the people were all amazed at the mighty power of God. And when they were come into the house, the disciples asked their Master why they could not cast out the unclean spirit. Jesus replied, This kind goeth not out by prayer and fasting.

Our Lord now spoke more plainly than ever to his disciples about his betrayal into the hands of his enemies, and his death and resurrection. But they did not understand him, and were afraid to ask what he meant. As they journeyed through Galilee the disciples disputed as to which of them should be greatest in the kingdom of heaven. When they reached Capernaum, Jesus asked what they had disputed about; but they held their peace. Jesus sat down, and taking a little child in his arms, he said, Except ye be converted, and become as little children, ye shall not enter into the kingdom of heaven. Whosoever therefore shall humble himself as this little child, the same is greatest in the kingdom of heaven.

At Capernaum our Lord seems to have devoted his time to teaching his disciples, and fitting them for the work that lay before them.

The feast of tabernacles was now at hand,

and the brethren of Jesus urged him to go up to it, that he might show them his mighty works, but none spake openly of him for fear of the Jews. But Jesus bade them go to the feast alone, for his time was not yet come. After his brethren had gone to the feast he also went up, but secretly. The Jews were looking out for him, and there was much murmuring among the people concerning him, some saying, He is a good man; others, Nay, but he deceiveth the people; for they did not yet believe on him.

At length Jesus appeared, and went into the temple and taught the people, saying, Ye both know me, and ye know whence I am; and I am not come of myself, but he that hath sent me is true, whom ye know not. But I know him: for I am from him, and he hath sent me. Then the people sought to take him; but his hour was not yet come.

The feast lasted eight days, and the last day was the great day, for then all the people assembled before returning to their homes. On that day Jesus stood up in the temple, and cried, If any man thirst, let him come unto me and drink. He here spoke of the living water of which he had spoken to the woman of Samaria. Then many of the people said, He is the Prophet; others, He is the Christ. The people were divided regarding him, and some would have taken him, but no man laid hands on him; while the officers who were sent by the Pharisees returned, excusing themselves by saying, Never man spake like this man.

Nicodemus pointed out to the Pharisees that the law judged no man till it heard him, but was met by the sneering reply, Art thou also of Galilee? Search and look, for out of Galilee ariseth no prophet.

Then the Pharisees became more bitter, putting many ensnaring questions to him, and trying hard to find something against him that they might accuse him. But he rebuked them for their unbelief, and told them that Abraham through faith believed upon him. They said, Thou art not yet fifty years old, and hast thou seen Abraham? Jesus replied, Verily, verily, I say unto you, Before Abraham was, I am. The Pharisees took up stones to stone him; but Jesus hid himself, and went out of the temple, going through the midst of them. And as he passed by he saw a man who had been blind from his birth. And his disciples asked him who did sin, this man or his parents? Jesus answered, Neither hath this man sinned, nor his parents: but that the works of God should be made manifest in him. I must work the works of him that sent me while it is day; the night cometh, when no man can work. As long as I am in the world, I am the light of the world. When he had thus spoken he anointed the eyes of the man with clay, and bade him go and wash in the pool of Siloam. He went and washed, and his sight returned. This happened on the Sabbath day.

The Pharisees, irritated at Jesus escaping from them, were still more angry when this man was brought before them upon whom such a wonderful miracle had been wrought. In their bitterness they could only say, This man is not of God, because he keepeth not the Sabbath day. They asked the man what he thought of him who had restored his sight; and he at once answered, He is a prophet. Upon this they pretended not to believe that he had been born blind, and called his parents to question them. Afraid to give offence, they said they could not answer; but their son was of age, he could speak for himself. Then the Pharisees told the man to give God the glory; as for Jesus, he was a sinner. But he boldly said, If this man were not of God, he could do nothing. In the end they cast him out of the synagogue, a most serious penalty, as it deprived him of his rights as a Jew, and made him an outcast from his father's house.

When Jesus heard of this, he sought the man out. And when he had found him, he said unto him, Dost thou believe on the Son of God? He answered and said, Who is he, Lord, that I might believe on him? And Jesus said unto him, Thou hast both seen him, and it is he that talketh with thee. And he said, Lord, I believe. And he worshipped him.

One day a lawyer asked Jesus this question, tempting him: Master, what shall I do to inherit eternal life? Jesus asked him what was written in the law; to which he replied, Thou shalt love the Lord thy God with all thy heart, and with all thy soul, and with all thy strength, and with all thy mind; and thy neighbor as thyself. Jesus said, Thou hast answered right; this do, and thou shalt live. The lawyer, willing to justify himself, asked who was his neighbor. Our Lord answered him by a parable: A certain man went down from Jerusalem to Jericho, and fell among thieves, who stripped him of his raiment, and wounded him, and departed, leaving him half dead. And by chance there came down a certain priest that way: and when he saw him, he passed by on the other side. And likewise a Levite, when he was at the place, came and looked on him, and passed by on the other side. But a certain Samaritan, as he journeyed, came where he was: and when he saw him, he had compassion on him, and went to him, and bound up his wounds, pouring in oil and wine, and set him on his own beast and brought him to an inn, and took care of him. And on the morrow when he departed, he took out two pence, and gave them to the host, and said unto him, Take care of him; and whatsoever thou spendest more, when I come again, I will repay thee. Which now of these three, thinkest thou, was neighbor unto him that fell among the thieves? And the lawyer said, He that showed mercy on him. Then said Jesus unto him, Go, and do thou likewise.

Two miles from Jerusalem, on the southeastern slope of the Mount of Olives, lay the small village of Bethany. There lived in this village three disciples of Jesus, Lazarus and his sisters Martha and Mary. Jesus, on one occasion, passed through the village, and Martha received him into the house. While Jesus spake unto them Mary sat at his feet and listened to his words, while Martha went about her household duties in an anxious mood. At length she came to the Lord, and asked him that he should tell her sister to come and help her. His answer was a gentle rebuke: Martha, Martha, he said, thou art careful and troubled about many things, but one thing is needful; and Mary has chosen that good part, which shall not be taken away from her.

One day, as Jesus was praying in a certain place, when he had ceased, one of the disciples requested that he should teach them to pray, as John taught his disciples. And he said unto them, When ye pray, say: Our Father, which art in heaven, hallowed be thy name: thy kingdom come: thy will be done, as in heaven, so in earth. Give us day by day our daily bread: and forgive us our sins; for we also forgive every one that is indebted to us. And lead us not into temptation: but deliver us from evil. At this time drew near unto Jesus all the Publicans and sinners to hear him, and the Pharisees and Scribes murmured, saying, This man receiveth sinners, and eateth with them. Jesus therefore spoke unto them this parable:

A certain man had two sons: and the younger of them said to his father, Father, give me the portion of goods that falleth to me. And he divided unto them his living. And not many days after, the younger son gathered all together, and took his journey into a far country, and there wasted his substance with riotous living. And when he had spent all, there arose a mighty famine in that land, and he began to be in want. And he went and joined himself to a citizen of that country; and he sent him into his fields to feed swine. And he would fain have filled his belly with the husks that the swine did eat: and no man gave unto him. And when he came to himself, he said, How many hired servants of my father's have bread enough and to spare, and I

THE RETURN OF THE PRODIGAL SON.

perish with hunger! I will arise and go to my father, and will say unto him, Father, I have sinned against heaven, and before thee, and am no more worthy to be called thy son: make me as one of thy hired servants. And he arose, and came to his father. But when he was yet a great way off, his father saw him, and had compassion, and ran, and fell on his neck, and kissed him. And the son said unto him, Father, I have sinned against heaven, and in thy sight, and am no more worthy to be called thy son. But the father said to his servants, Bring forth the best robe, and put it on him; and put a ring on his hand, and shoes on his feet: and bring hither the fatted calf, and kill it; and let us eat, and be merry: for this my son was dead, and is alive again; he was lost, and is found. And they began to be merry. Now his elder son was in the field: and as he came and drew nigh to the house, he heard music and dancing. And he called one of the servants, and asked what these things meant. And he said unto him, Thy brother is come; and thy father hath killed the fatted calf, because he hath received him safe and sound. And he was angry, and would not go in; therefore came his father out, and entreated him. And he, answering, said to his father, Lo, these many years do I serve thee, neither transgressed I at any time thy commandment: and yet thou never gavest me a kid, that I might make merry with my friends; but as soon as this thy son was come, which hath devoured thy living with harlots, thou hast killed for him the fatted calf. And he said unto him, Son, thou art ever with me, and all that I have is thine. It was meet that we should make merry, and be glad: for this thy brother was dead, and is alive again; and was lost, and is found.

CHAPTER VII

THE PARABLE OF THE RICH MAN AND LAZARUS—OF THE PHARISEE AND THE PUBLICAN—THE RAISING OF LAZARUS—BLIND BARTIMEUS HEALED—THE CALLING OF ZACCHEUS—CHRIST'S ENTRY INTO JERUSALEM—HE TEACHES IN THE TEMPLE—THE PARABLE OF THE TEN VIRGINS.

OUR Lord spoke another parable to those who were covetous and lovers of money: There was a certain rich man, which was clothed in purple and fine linen, and fared sumptuously every day: and there was a certain beggar named Lazarus, which was laid at his gate, full of sores, and desiring to be fed with the crumbs which fell from the rich man's table: moreover the dogs came and licked his sores. And it came to pass that the beggar died, and was carried by the angels into Abraham's bosom: the rich man also died, and was buried; and in hell he lifted up his eyes, being in torments, and seeth Abraham afar off, and Lazarus in his bosom. And he cried and said, Father Abraham, have mercy on me, and send Lazarus, that he may dip the tip of his finger in water, and cool my tongue, for I am tormented in this flame. But Abraham said, Son, remember that thou in thy lifetime receivedst the good things, and likewise Lazarus evil things: but now he is comforted, and thou art tormented. And beside all this, between us and you there is a great gulf fixed: so that they which would pass from hence to you cannot; neither can they pass to us that would come from thence. Then he said, I pray thee therefore, father, that thou wouldest send him to my father's house: for I have five brethren; that he may testify unto them, lest they also come into this place of torment. Abraham saith unto him, They have Moses and the prophets; let them hear them. And he said, Nay, father Abraham: but if one went unto them from the dead, they will repent. And he said unto him, If they hear not Moses and the prophets, neither will they be persuaded though one rose from the dead.

And Jesus spoke another parable to those who thought themselves righteous and despised others: Two men went up into the temple to pray; the one a Pharisee, and the other a Publican. The Pharisee stood and prayed thus with himself: God, I thank thee that I am not as other men are, extortioners, unjust, adulterers, or even as this Publican. I fast twice in the week, I give tithes of all that I possess. And the Publican, standing afar off, would not lift so much as his eyes unto heaven, but smote upon his breast, saying, God be merciful to me a sinner. I tell you, this man went down to his house justified rather than the other: for every one that exalteth himself shall be abased, and he that humbleth himself shall be exalted.

And women brought their little children to Jesus that he might put his hands on them, and bless them, but the disciples rebuked them. Then Jesus called them

BLESSING THE CHILDREN

unto him, saying, Suffer the little children to come unto me, and forbid them not; for of such is the kingdom of God.

And at the feast of the dedication Jesus walked in Solomon's porch, in the temple, when some of the Jews asked him to tell them plainly whether he were the Christ or not. Jesus replied that the works he had done in his Father's name were his witness.

Jesus therefore left Jerusalem, and retired beyond the river Jordan, to the place where John had baptized. And many believed on him there. While he was in this place, a messenger arrived from the sisters of Bethany, Martha and Mary, to tell Jesus that their brother Lazarus was sick. Now, although Jesus loved Martha and her sister, and Lazarus, he did not at once depart, but remained where he was two days longer. Then he said to his disciples, Let us go into Judea again. They remonstrated, reminding him that his life was in danger; but he told them no harm would come to him until the appointed time. He then told them Lazarus was dead, adding, I am glad for your sakes I was not there, to the intent ye might believe. So they went to Bethany, and on arriving there found that Lazarus had been already four days in the grave. When the news reached Martha that Jesus was not far off, she rose up and went to meet him. When she met him, she fell at his feet, and said, Lord, If thou hadst been here, my brother had not died. But I know that even now, whatsoever thou wilt ask of God, God will give it thee. Jesus said to her, Thy brother shall rise again. Martha replied, I know that he shall rise again in the resurrection at the last day. Jesus said unto her, I

RAISING LAZARUS FROM THE DEAD

am the resurrection and the life: he that believeth in me, though he were dead, yet shall he live: and whosoever liveth and believeth in me shall never die. Believest thou this? She said unto him, Yea, Lord; I believe that thou art the Christ, the Son of God, which should come into the world. When she had so said she went and said to her sister secretly, The Master is come, and calleth for thee. Mary rose quickly and went out, and the friends who were with her, thinking she had gone to the grave to weep there, followed her. On meeting Jesus, Mary also fell at his feet, and said, Lord, if thou hadst been here, my brother had not died. When our Lord saw Mary and the friends that were with her weeping, he was troubled, and we are told that "Jesus wept." Then said the people, Behold how he loved him! When they were come to the grave, Jesus bade them take away the stone. Martha reminded him that he had been dead four days, but Jesus answered, Said I not unto thee that, if thou wouldest believe, thou shouldest see the glory of God? Then they took away the stone from the place where the dead was laid. And Jesus lifted up his eyes, and said, Father, I thank thee that thou hast heard me. And I knew that thou hearest me always: but because of the people which stand by I said it, that they may believe that thou hast sent me. And when he thus had spoken, he cried with a loud voice, Lazarus, come forth! At the sound of that voice Lazarus came forth, and Jesus bade those who stood around loose him from his grave-clothes and let him go.

And many of the Jews which had seen these things

believed on Jesus; but others hastened to Jerusalem and told the Pharisees what they had seen. From that time the chief priests and Pharisees determined that he should be put to death. But Jesus went with his disciples into a country near to the wilderness, into a city called Ephraim, and there abode. Their plots, therefore, had to be deferred until the approaching Passover, now near at hand, when they hoped that Jesus would come to the feast, and then they would be able to compass his death.

Jesus, knowing his time had now come, left his quiet retreat, and joined the stream of pilgrims who were wending their way towards Jerusalem. Again, for the third time, he told his disciples more plainly than ever what treatment he should receive at Jerusalem: how he would be mocked, scourged, spat upon, and finally be crucified and laid in the grave, but on the third day he would rise again. Even yet the disciples failed to comprehend the full import of these words, for shortly after we find the mother of James and John asking Jesus that her sons might sit, the one at his right hand, and the other at his left, when he came into his kingdom.

Travelling onwards, the twelve, with their Master, reached the city of Jericho. Somewhere in the neighborhood, by the wayside, sat a blind beggar named Bartimeus. When he heard the noise of the passing crowd, he inquired what was the matter. On being told that Jesus of Nazareth passed by, he cried with a loud voice, Jesus, thou Son of David, have mercy on me. And they which went before rebuked him that he should hold his peace; but he cried so much the more, Thou Son of David, have mercy on me. Jesus hearing the cry, stopped, and asked Bartimeus what he would do for him. He answered, Lord, that I may receive my sight. And Jesus touched his eyes, and told him to go, for his faith had saved him; and immediately he received his sight and followed Jesus.

While passing through Jericho, a rich Publican named Zaccheus was very anxious to see Jesus, but could not for the crowd, because he was very short of stature. And he ran before, and climbed up a tree, and when Jesus came to the place, he looked up, and said, Zaccheus, make haste and come down, for to-day I must abide at thy house. Joyfully Zaccheus responded to the call, and welcomed Jesus to his home. But the people murmured because he was the guest of one of the hated tax-gatherers. Zaccheus said to the Lord, Behold, Lord, the half of my goods I give to the poor; and if I have taken anything from any man by false accusation, I restore him fourfold. Jesus said to him, This day is salvation come to this house, forasmuch as he also is a son of Abraham. For the Son of Man is come to seek and to save that which was lost.

Proceeding towards Jerusalem, our Lord reached Bethany two days before the Passover, and there a feast was given in his honor in the house of Simon the leper. Martha was present serving, but Lazarus, who had been raised from the dead, sat at the table with Jesus. Then Mary, who was there also, took a box of costly ointment, and anointed the feet of Jesus, and wiped them with her hair. And the house was filled with the odor of the ointment. Then said Judas, who was afterwards to betray him,

JESUS CALLING ZACCHEUS DOWN FROM THE TREE.

Why was not this ointment sold, and the price given to the poor? Then said Jesus, Let her alone, against the day of my burying hath she done this. For the poor ye have with you always; but me ye have not always.

The next day Jesus proceeded to Jerusalem; and as he came near the village of Bethpage, he sent two of the disciples before him, telling them that as they entered the village they would find a colt tied, which no one had ever ridden. This colt they were to bring to him, and if the owners objected, they were to say, The Lord hath need of him. And the disciples brought the colt to him, and throwing their garments over, they set him thereon. And some of the people spread their garments, while others cut down branches and strewed them in the way. And the multitudes shouted, Hosanna to the Son of David! Blessed is he that cometh in the name of the Lord, Hosanna in the highest.

And when Jesus approached Jerusalem and beheld the city, he wept over it. He not only wept, but broke into a passion of lamentation, saying, If thou hadst known, even thou, at least in this thy day, the things that belong unto thy peace! but now they are hid from thine eyes. For the days shall come upon thee, that thine enemies shall cast a trench about thee, and compass thee round, and keep thee in on every side, and shall lay thee even with the ground, and thy children within thee; and they shall not leave in thee one stone upon another; because thou knewest not the time of thy visitation.

And as Jesus entered Jerusalem, the whole city

THE ENTRY INTO JERUSALEM

was moved, and the people asked, Who is this? And the multitude answered, This is Jesus the prophet of Nazareth of Galilee. He went into the temple, and as three years before he had purged it, so now again he cast out the money-changers and those who sold doves, saying, It is written, My house is the house of prayer; but ye have made it a den of thieves. And the blind and the lame came to Jesus, and he healed them; and the children shouted, Hosanna to the Son of David, which made the priests and the Scribes come to him and ask in deep displeasure, Hearest thou what these say? Yea, was the answer; have ye never read, Out of the mouths of babes and sucklings thou hast perfected praise?

And he spoke daily in the temple at this time, teaching the people in parables; and the Pharisees, seeing the deep impression his words made upon them, tried to catch him in his words, and for this purpose sent different persons to try him with hard questions, in the hope that his answers might offend the people, and turn them against him. The Sadducees also came to Jesus asking questions and hoping that they might draw from his reply something to bring against him. But by the wisdom of his answers he silenced them all.

The Lord then, in the hearing of all the people, warned his disciples, and bade them beware of the Scribes and Pharisees. Their religion was a mere pretence; they were proud, and liked to receive great honor, and therefore they made long prayers; but their deeds were evil, and their condemnation would be the greater.

Four of the disciples came privately to Jesus, and asked him to tell them what would be the signs of his coming and of the end of the world, and when these things should happen. But Jesus told them that only God the Father knew that. Ye must therefore, he added, take heed, and watch and pray, for ye know not when the time is. Jesus then uttered this parable of the ten virgins, to impress yet more deeply upon their minds the necessity of watchfulness and faithfulness: Then shall the kingdom of heaven be likened unto ten virgins, which took their lamps, and went forth to meet the bridegroom. And five of them were wise, and five were foolish. They that were foolish took their lamps, and took no oil with them: but the wise took oil in their vessels with their lamps. While the bridegroom tarried, they all slumbered and slept. And at midnight there was a cry made, Behold, the bridegroom cometh; go ye out to meet him. Then all those virgins arose, and trimmed their lamps. And the foolish said unto the wise, Give us of your oil; for our lamps are gone out. But the wise answered, saying, Not so; lest there be not enough for us and you: but go ye rather to them that sell, and buy for yourselves. And while they went to buy, the bridegroom came; and they that were ready went in with him to the marriage: and the door was shut. Afterward came also the other virgins, saying, Lord, Lord, open to us. But he answered and said, Verily I say unto you, I know you not. Watch, therefore, for ye know neither the day nor the hour wherein the Son of Man cometh.

CHAPTER VIII

JUDAS SELLS HIS MASTER—JESUS OBSERVES THE PASSOVER, AND INSTITUTES THE HOLY SUPPER—HE COMFORTS HIS DISCIPLES—THE AGONY IN GETHSEMANE—JESUS IS CARRIED BEFORE CAIAPHAS—HE IS DELIVERED BOUND TO PILATE—HE SENDS HIM TO HEROD—HEROD INSULTS HIM AND SENDS HIM BACK TO PILATE—HE IS CRUCIFIED, AND IS BURIED IN THE TOMB OF JOSEPH OF ARIMATHEA.

MEANWHILE the enemies of Jesus, baffled in their attempts to ensnare him by their questions, met together to consider how he might be taken by craft and killed. This they saw they could not do publicly, on the feast day, for fear of an uproar among the people. While they were discussing the matter, Judas Iscariot, one of the twelve, came to them, and offered to betray his Master. They at once accepted his offer, and agreed to pay him thirty pieces of silver.

On the first day of the feast of the Passover the disciples of Jesus asked him where he meant to keep the feast. And he said, Go into the city to such a man, and say unto him, The Master saith, My time is at hand; I will keep the Passover at thy house with my disciples. And the disciples did as Jesus had appointed them; and they made ready the Passover.

When evening was come Jesus entered the city and proceeded to the large upper chamber where

THE LORD'S SUPPER.

the feast was prepared, and sat down with the twelve. And as he did eat he spoke of his betrayal, saying that one of them would betray him to his enemies. And they were exceedingly sorrowful, and began every one to ask, Lord, is it I? Jesus replied, He it is to whom I shall give a sop when I have dipped it. And when he had dipped the sop he gave it to Judas Iscariot.

And as they were eating, Jesus took bread, and blessed it, and broke it, and gave it to the disciples, and said, Take, eat; this is my body. And he took the cup, and gave thanks, and gave it to them, saying, Drink ye all of it: for this is my blood of the new testament, which is shed for many for the remission of sins.

Then Jesus addressed unto his disciples those beautiful and comforting words, preserved to us in St. John's gospel, beginning with, "Let not your heart be troubled; ye believe in God, believe also in me."

Then he prayed, and after they had sung an hymn, our Lord, with the eleven faithful apostles, came to the Mount of Olives, and then made their way to an olive grove called Gethsemane. Here our Lord, telling the rest of the disciples to sit down, took with him Peter, James, and John, and retired to pray. And he began to be very sorrowful and heavy, and he said to them, My soul is exceeding sorrowful, even unto death: tarry ye here, and watch with me. And he withdrew about a stone's cast and knelt down and prayed. And being in an agony, he prayed more earnestly, and his sweat was, as it were, great drops of blood, falling to the ground. And the

GETHSEMANE

burden of his prayer to his Father was that the cup of sorrow might pass from him, but he added, Nevertheless not what I will, but what thou wilt. It was not the Father's will that the cup of suffering should be removed; but he prepared him for it, for an angel appeared from heaven, and strengthened him. When Jesus returned to his disciples, he found them asleep. Waking them, he said, Rise, let us go; lo, he that betrayeth me is at hand. While he yet spake, there came Judas, one of the twelve, and with him a multitude with swords and clubs, whom the chief priests, Scribes, and elders had sent out to do his bidding. Judas had said to these soldiers, Whomsoever I kiss, that is he. Take him, and lead him away safely.

When he came unto the garden, he went straightway to Jesus, saying, Rabbi, rabbi, and drew near to kiss him. Jesus saith unto him, Judas, betrayeth thou the Son of Man with a kiss? Then as the men came near with their lanterns and torches, Jesus said unto them, Whom seek ye? And they said, Jesus of Nazareth. Jesus said unto them, I am he.

As the armed men closed around Jesus, the disciples drew back, fearing to stay by him lest they also should be seized and put in prison. So they all forsook him and fled.

Jesus was then led to the house of Caiaphas, the high priest, where the Scribes and elders were assembled. Here he was examined and subjected to much insult.

Witnesses were brought to speak against him, but their statements did not agree one with another. But Jesus held his peace. At last Caiaphas stood

JUDAS BETRAYS JESUS WITH A KISS

up and asked him to tell them if he were the Christ, the
Son of God. And Jesus said, I am, and ye shall see
the Son of Man sitting on the right hand of power,
and coming in the clouds of heaven. This was
enough. Caiaphas rent his clothes, saying, What
need have we of any further witnesses? Ye have
heard the blasphemy: what think ye? And they all
with one consent pronounced him worthy of death.
And they began to spit on him, and to strike him
with the palms of their hands.

Next morning they took Jesus and bound him,
and led him away and delivered him to Pontius
Pilate, the Roman governor, to be judged by him.
They themselves could not enter Pilate's judgment
hall for fear of being defiled, and thus rendered unfit
to eat the Passover. Pilate therefore went out to
them, and asked what they had to accuse Jesus of?
They replied, that if he had not been a malefactor
they would not have brought him. Take ye him,
said Pilate, and judge him according to your law.
They answered, It is not lawful for us to put any
man to death. Then Pilate returned to the judgment hall, and asked Jesus, Art thou the King of
the Jews? Jesus answered, My kingdom is not of
this world. If my kingdom were of this world, then
would my servants fight, that I should not be delivered to the Jews: but now is my kingdom not from
hence. Pilate therefore said unto him, Art thou a
king? Jesus answered, Thou sayest that I am a
king. To this end was I born, and for this cause
came I into the world, that I should bear witness
unto the truth. Every one that is of the truth
heareth my voice. Pilate asked, What is truth? but

JESUS BEFORE PILATE

not waiting for a reply, returned to the Jews, and said, I find in him no fault at all. He then reminded them that they had a custom whereby one prisoner was released at the Passover, and asked if he should release unto them Jesus. But they cried, Not this man, but Barabbas. Now Barabbas was a robber.

Eager to get rid of a prisoner he had no wish to condemn, Pilate, hearing from the Jews that Galilee had been the chief scene of Jesus' ministry, sent him to Herod, under whose jurisdiction Galilee was. When Herod saw Jesus he was glad, for he hoped to witness some miracle performed by him. To all the many questions Herod put to Jesus, even though the chief priests stood by accusing him, he answered not a word. Then Herod, with his soldiers, arrayed Jesus in a gorgeous robe and mocked him. When he had done this he sent him back to Pilate.

Pilate was troubled by the return of the prisoner and his accusers; and calling together the chief priests and elders, he told them that he, and Herod also, had examined Jesus, and nothing worthy of death could be found in him. I will therefore chastise him, and let him go, he said. But they cried, saying, Crucify him! crucify him!

Pilate now became more desirous than ever to release Jesus, asking the people what evil he had done, but the Jews cried out the more, If thou let this man go, thou art not Cæsar's friend: whosoever maketh himself a king speaketh against Cæsar. When Pilate heard the name of Cæsar, he brought Jesus forth, and he said to the people, Shall I crucify your king? The chief priests answered, We have

JESUS CARRIES HIS CROSS

no king but Cæsar. Pilate then, in presence of the people, took water and washed his hands, and said, I am innocent of the blood of this just person: see ye to it. Then answered all the people, His blood be on us and on our children. And Pilate gave sentence that it should be as they required. Pilate now delivered Jesus up to them, and they scourged him, and platted a crown of thorns, and put it on his head, and put a reed for a sceptre in his hand, and bowing the knee before him, mocked him, crying, Hail, King of the Jews! And they spat upon him, and took the reed, and smote him upon the head. They then led him out to crucify him, and they took hold of a man named Simon, a native of Cyrene, and on him they laid the cross that he might bear it after Jesus. And a great crowd followed Jesus, and many women, who bewailed and lamented him. But Jesus turned to them, and said, Daughters of Jerusalem, weep not for me, but weep for yourselves, and for your children.

And when they were come to the place called Calvary, which was just beyond the city walls, they nailed him to the cross, and crucified him, and at the same time two thieves, one on the right hand, and the other on the left. Then said Jesus, Father, forgive them; for they know not what they do. And they that passed by reviled him, wagging their heads, and saying, If thou be the Son of God, come down from the cross. And the people stood beholding him, and with their rulers mocked and derided him, saying, He saved others; himself he cannot save. The soldiers also mocked him, offering him vinegar to drink, and saying, If thou be the king of

THE CRUCIFIXION

the Jews, save thyself. And even one of the thieves railed on him, asking him to save himself and them; but the other rebuked his companion, reminding him that they were only receiving the just reward of their deeds, but that Jesus had done nothing amiss. And Jesus said to him, To-day thou shalt be with me in paradise.

And Mary, the mother of Jesus, was standing by, with her sister Mary, the wife of Cleophas, and Mary Magdalene; also John, the beloved disciple. When Jesus beheld his mother and the disciple standing by whom he loved, he said to his mother, Woman, behold thy son, and to the disciple, Behold thy mother.

About noon the sky became very dark, and for three hours there was darkness over all the land. And about the ninth hour Jesus cried with a loud voice, My God, my God, why hast thou forsaken me? After this he said, I thirst. And one ran and filled a sponge with vinegar, and gave it to him to drink. When he had received the vinegar, he commended his spirit to his Father, and with the words, It is finished, he bowed his head, and gave up the ghost. At that moment the veil of the temple was rent in two, from the top to the bottom; and the earth trembled, and the rocks were rent; and the graves were opened, and gave forth their dead.

And the captain of the Roman soldiers who stood by said, Truly this man was the Son of God. The next day, being the Sabbath day, the Jews went to Pilate and besought him that the legs of the crucified might be broken, and the bodies taken down. The soldiers therefore broke the legs of the two thieves, who were still alive; but finding that Jesus was already dead, they broke not his legs, that the Scripture might be fulfilled, A bone of him shall not be broken. One of the soldiers, however, thrust his spear into Jesus' side, thus fulfilling another prophecy, They shall look on him whom they pierced.

And one of the disciples, Joseph of Arimathea, a rich man, went to Pilate secretly and besought him that he might take away the body of Jesus. And Pilate having given him leave, he took the body from the cross, and wrapped it in fine linen, with costly spices, which had been brought by Nicodemus. And near where he was crucified there was a garden, and in it a new sepulchre, wherein man had never been laid; and here they laid Jesus. And Mary Magdalene and other women from Galilee were watching, and saw where Jesus was buried; then they returned to the city to prepare spices and ointments to anoint the body when the Sabbath day was over.

The Pharisees meanwhile, remembering the words Jesus had uttered regarding his resurrection, went to Pilate pretending they were afraid lest his disciples might steal the body, and begged that a watch might be set over the grave until the third day. This permission being granted, they went, and made the sepulchre sure, sealing the stone, and setting a watch thereon.

CHAPTER IX

THE WOMEN FIND THE TOMB EMPTY—TWO ANGELS APPEAR TO THEM, AND TELL THEM "HE IS RISEN"—APPEARS TO MARY MAGDALENE, TO TWO DISCIPLES ON THE WAY TO EMMAUS, AND TO THE OTHER DISCIPLES—HE BLESSES THEM, AND ASCENDS TO HEAVEN—THE FEAST OF PENTECOST —THE MARTYRDOM OF STEPHEN—THE CONVERSION OF PAUL—PAUL'S MISSIONARY JOURNEY— THE SPREAD OF THE GOSPEL—EPISTLES TO THE CHURCHES—THE REVELATION OF JOHN.

AND when Mary Magdalene and the other women came very early in the morning of the first day of the week with spices to anoint the body of Jesus, they found that there had been a great earthquake, the stone had been rolled back from the door, and the grave was empty. And behold an angel of the Lord sat upon the stone, and his countenance was like lightning, and his raiment white as snow. And the angel said to the women, Fear not ye; for I know that ye seek Jesus, which was crucified. He is not here: for he has risen, as he said. Come, see the place where the Lord lay: and go quickly and tell his disciples that he is risen from the dead; and, behold, he goeth before you into Galilee; there shall ye see him; lo, I have told you.

The women, trembling with fear and joy, hastened away to tell the disciples, and as they went Jesus met them, and said, All hail. And they held him

THE RESURRECTION

by the feet, and worshipped him, while Jesus told them not to be afraid, and repeated the message the angel had given them. And they came to the disciples and told them, but some of them did not believe the glad news. Peter and John, however, hastened to the grave, and John, outstripping Peter, arrived first, and looking into the open grave, he found it empty, save for the linen garments which lay neatly folded; but he did not go in. When Peter came up, he entered the sepulchre, and saw the linen clothes in which the dead body of Jesus had been wrapped. John now entered, and they both believed, for until then they had not understood that Jesus must rise again from the dead. They then returned to their own home.

But Mary Magdalene stood without at the sepulchre weeping, and looking in she saw two shining ones, who asked her why she wept. She said, Because they have taken away my Lord, and I know not where they have laid him. Turning away, she beheld Jesus standing beside her, but she knew him not. Imagining him to be the gardener, she said to him: Sir, if thou have borne him hence, tell me where thou hast laid him, and I will take him away. Jesus said to her, Mary. In an instant her eyes were opened, she knew her risen Lord, and she cried, Rabboni; which is to say, Master. But Jesus said, Touch me not; for I am not yet ascended to my Father; but go to my brethren, and say unto them, I ascend unto my Father, and your Father; and to my God, and your God. Then Mary went and told the disciples that she had seen the Lord.

The soldiers who had been watching the grave

HE IS RISEN

now went to the chief priests and told them all that had been done. They immediately assembled with the elders, and consulted how they might get the people to disbelieve the resurrection. They therefore bribed the soldiers to spread the report that the disciples of Jesus had come by night, and stole him away while they slept.

That same day, as two of the disciples were walking toward Emmaus, talking of all that had happened during the last few days, a stranger joined them, who asked them why they looked so sad. They in turn asked him how he could be ignorant of the things that had lately taken place in Jerusalem. And he said unto them, What things? They then told him about Jesus of Nazareth, a prophet mighty in deed and word, who they trusted would have redeemed Israel, but who had been condemned by the chief priests and crucified, and who it was rumored had now risen from the dead. Then their fellow-traveller said to them, Ought not Christ to have suffered these things, and to enter into his glory? And beginning at Moses and all the prophets, he expounded unto them in all the Scriptures the things concerning himself.

As they talked, they reached Emmaus, and the disciples constrained him, saying, Abide with us: for it is toward evening, and the day is far spent. He consented, and as they sat down to their evening meal, he took the bread and blessed it; then they recognized their Lord, but even as they did so he departed out of their sight. Then they said one to another, Did not our heart burn within us while he talked to us by the way, and while he opened to us

THE INCREDULITY OF THOMAS

the Scriptures? They rose at once, and returned to Jerusalem with the glad news, telling the things that happened in the way, and how he was known of them in breaking of bread. The same day at evening the risen Lord appeared again to his disciples, who were assembled with closed doors for fear of the Jews, and he stood in the midst of them, and said, Peace be with you. When the apostle Thomas, who was not present, was told of this, he said, Except I shall see in his hands the prints of the nails, and put my finger into the print of the nails, and thrust my hand into his side, I will not believe.

A week passed, and the disciples were again met together with closed doors, when Jesus appeared among them. After blessing them, he called on Thomas to reach forth his finger, and put it in the print of the nails, and to thrust his hand into the wound in his side, and to be not faithless, but believing. And Thomas answered and said, My Lord and my God. Jesus said, Because thou hast seen me, thou hast believed: blessed are they that have not seen, and yet have believed.

In obedience to the command of Jesus, the disciples had proceeded north to Galilee, and his next appearance was to seven of them who had gone out fishing upon the lake. All night they had toiled, and caught nothing. At dawn they saw one standing on the shore, who asked if they had caught anything. They answered, No. He bade them cast the net on the right side of the ship, and they would find. They did so, and could scarcely draw in the net for the multitude of fishes. Therefore that disciple whom Jesus loved said to Peter, It is the Lord.

JESUS APPEARS TO HIS DISCIPLES.

Peter cast himself into the water, and swam ashore. When the others landed, dragging the net, they found a fire burning on the shore, and some fish cooking with bread beside it. Jesus bade them bring fish of the which they had caught, and then come and dine. And he divided the bread and fish amongst them.

When the meal was over, Jesus asked Peter three times, Lovest thou me? And Peter was vexed when Jesus had asked him the third time, and he said, Lord, thou knowest all things; thou knowest that I love thee. Then Jesus said, Feed my lambs; feed my sheep.

It may have been at this time that Jesus appointed his disciples to meet him on a mountain in Galilee. About five hundred saw the Lord on this occasion, and worshipped him, and received from him his last commands. He ordered them to go and teach all nations, baptizing them in the name of the Father, and of the Son, and of the Holy Ghost; and he promised that he would be with them always, even to the end of the world. Jesus remained upon earth for forty days after the resurrection; but the time had now come when he must leave, not to return until he comes in glory to judge the world. He met his disciples once more in Jerusalem, and leading them out as far as Bethany, he lifted up his hands, and blessed them, and as he did so he was parted from them, and a cloud received him out of their sight.

After our Lord's ascension the disciples returned to Jerusalem, and abode in an upper room, where they prayed and gave thanks along with the faithful

THE ASCENSION INTO HEAVEN

women, and Mary the mother of Jesus, and his brethren. Ten days after came the feast of Pentecost, and on the first day of this feast the disciples were all in one place, when suddenly there came a sound from heaven as of a rushing mighty wind, and it filled all the house where they were sitting. And there appeared cloven tongues as of fire resting on the head of each of them. And they were filled with the Holy Ghost, and began to speak with other tongues. And there were at that time dwelling at Jerusalem devout men out of every nation under heaven. And when every man heard the apostles speak in his own language they were amazed and confounded, and some mocked and said, These men are full of new wine. But Peter, standing up, lifted up his voice, and preached to them of Jesus of Nazareth—how his coming had been foretold by the prophets—how, when he did come, he was taken by the Jews, and crucified and slain—how God had raised him up, whereof they were all witnesses—and concluded by showing them that God had made that same Jesus both Lord and Christ. When they heard this, they were pricked in their heart, and said, Men and brethren, what shall we do? Then Peter said unto them, Repent, and be baptized every one of you in the name of Jesus Christ for the remission of sins, and ye shall receive the gift of the Holy Ghost. Then they that gladly received his word were baptized: and the same day there were added unto them about three thousand souls. And they continued steadfastly in the apostles' doctrine and fellowship, and in breaking of bread, and in prayers. And all that believed were together, and had all things common; and they, continuing daily with one accord in the temple, and breaking bread from house to house, did eat their meat with gladness and singleness of heart, praising God, and having favor with all the people.

And so the faith of Jesus spread, but the hatred of his enemies broke out once more.

Their first victim was Stephen, a man full of faith and of the Holy Ghost, who did many wonderful miracles. False accusations were brought against him, but being permitted to answer them, his enemies were so enraged by what he said, that they gnashed on him with their teeth. But he, being full of the Holy Ghost, looked up steadfastly into heaven, and saw the glory of God, and Jesus standing on the right hand of God, and said, Behold, I see the heavens opened, and the Son of Man standing on the right hand of God. Then they cried out with a loud voice, and stopped their ears, and ran upon him with one accord, and cast him out of the city, and stoned him: and the witnesses laid down their clothes at a young man's feet, whose name was Saul. And they stoned Stephen calling upon God, and saying, Lord Jesus, receive my spirit. And he kneeled down, and cried with a loud voice, Lord, lay not this sin to their charge. And, when he had said this, he fell asleep.

Among those who were present at the stoning of Stephen there was a young man named Saul. He was a strict Pharisee, and had consented to Stephen's death, and had become a notable persecutor of the Church. Breathing out threatenings and slaughter against the disciples of the Lord, he started for

Damascus for the purpose of bringing back to Jerusalem, as prisoners, all the disciples of Jesus he could find in that city. As he drew near to it, suddenly a great light shone round about him, brighter than the noonday sun, and a voice was heard, saying, Saul, Saul, why persecutest thou me? Saul, who had fallen on his face, answered, Who art thou, Lord? And the voice replied, I am Jesus whom thou persecutest. And Saul was afraid, and asked, Lord, what wilt thou have me do? And the Lord said unto him, Arise, and go into the city, and it shall be told thee what thou must do. When Saul arose from the earth he could not see; and he was for three days without sight, and did neither eat nor drink; when one Ananias came to him. Now Ananias, who was a follower of Jesus, had been warned in a vision to go into a certain house, in a street called Straight, and inquire for one Saul of Tarsus, and lay his hand on him, that his sight might be restored. And when Ananias feared, because he had heard how Saul persecuted the Church, the Lord commanded him to go, for he had chosen Saul to bear his name before the Gentiles, and kings, and the children of Israel. Ananias obeyed, and came to the house, and laying his hands on Saul, said, Brother Saul, the Lord, even Jesus, that appeared unto thee in the way as thou camest, hath sent me, that thou mightest receive thy sight, and be filled with the Holy Ghost. And immediately Saul received his sight, and he arose and was baptized.

And straightway he preached Christ in the synagogues of Damascus. And all that heard him were amazed, and inquired whether this was not he who

THE CONVERSION OF PAUL

destroyed them that called on Christ at Jerusalem. But Saul increased the more in strength, and confounded the Jews, proving that this was very Christ. Then the Jews were filled with anger against him, and sought opportunity to kill him. The disciples hearing of this let him down over the city wall in a basket, by night, and he escaped out of their hands.

After this Saul is called Paul in Holy Scripture. He was eminently the apostle to the Gentiles. In his first missionary tour he was accompanied by Barnabas and his nephew John Mark. At this time they visited the island of Cyprus preaching the Christ, and also many towns on the mainland, notably Antioch, where they abode a long time with the disciples, who were first called Christians there. On their return to Jerusalem they were received by the apostles and elders and the whole Church, to whom they told all the wonderful things God had done by them among the Gentiles.

Paul and Barnabas afterwards returned to Antioch, accompanied by Judas, surnamed Barsabas, and Silas. When they had stayed some time in that city teaching and preaching, Paul proposed that they should revisit all the cities where they had already preached the Word of the Lord; but a dispute arose between him and Barnabas, and the contention was so sharp that they parted the one from the other. And Paul, taking Silas with him, went through Syria and Cilicia, visiting the churches.

And he came to Lystra, and here he found a young disciple named Timothy. From a child he had known the Scriptures, and Paul chose him to go with himself and Silas that he might preach the gospel.

And Paul came to Troas, and while there he had a wonderful vision. There stood a man of Macedonia, and prayed him, saying, Come over into Macedonia, and help us; and assuredly gathering from this that the Lord had called him to preach the gospel there, he sailed with those who were with him, and came to a city of Macedonia called Philippi.

At Philippi Paul and Silas were beaten, and then put in prison, with their feet in the stocks. And at midnight they prayed and sang praises to God. And suddenly there was a a great earthquake which shook the prison, and flung open the doors, and their chains fell off. And the keeper of the prison awaking out of his sleep, and seeing the prison doors open, would have put himself to death; but Paul and Silas called out to him to do himself no harm, as none of the prisoners had escaped. The jailer came trembling, and fell down before them, saying, Sirs, what must I do to be saved? And they said, Believe on the Lord Jesus Christ, and thou shalt be saved, and thy house.

The rest of Paul's life was full of perils by sea and by land. He made many missionary journeys through Greece and Syria, and coming to Jerusalem was made a prisoner and taken before Felix, the Roman governor of Judea. Paul defended himself before Felix, and as he reasoned of righteousness, temperance, and judgment to come, Felix trembled, and said, Go thy way for this time: when I have a convenient season I will hear thee. But he still kept Paul a prisoner, and when he was succeeded by another governor, named Festus, he left Paul to be dealt with by him. He was then brought before Festus, but he declared he had done the Jews no wrong, and being a Roman citizen, appealed unto Cæsar. Then King Agrippa came on a visit to Festus, and Paul was brought before them both. Agrippa said to Paul, Thou art permitted to speak for thyself. Paul began by complimenting the king on his knowledge of Jewish laws and customs, and then told the story of his life from his youth up, his miraculous conversion, and his call to be an apostle, concluding thus: Having therefore obtained help of God, I continue unto this day, witnessing both to small and great, saying none other things than those which the prophets and Moses did say should come; that Christ should suffer, and that he should be the first that should rise from the dead and should show light unto the people, and to the Gentiles.

And as he thus spake for himself, Festus said with a loud voice, Paul, thou art beside thyself; much learning doth make thee mad. But he said, I am not mad, most noble Festus; but speak forth the words of truth and soberness. For the king knoweth of these things, before whom also I speak freely: for I am persuaded that none of these things are hidden from him; for this thing was not done in a corner. King Agrippa, believest thou the prophets? I know that thou believest. Then Agrippa said unto Paul, Almost thou persuadest me to be a Christian. And Paul said, I would to God, that not only thou, but also all that hear me this day, were both almost, and altogether such as I am, except these bonds.

And when he had thus spoken, the king rose up, and the governor, and Bernice, and they that sat with them: and when they were gone aside, they talked between themselves, saying, This man doeth nothing worthy of death, or of bonds. Then said Agrippa unto Festus, This man might have been set at liberty, if he had not appealed unto Cæsar.

Paul was then sent with other prisoners to Rome, and suffered shipwreck on the way thither. But all in the ship escaped safe to land, which they found to be an island called Melita—now called Malta— the people of which showed great kindness to the shipwrecked strangers. After waiting here three months, they sailed again in a ship, which took them as far as Puteoli, whence they journeyed by land to Rome. And the Christians in Rome came to meet Paul outside the city; and when he saw them he thanked God, and took courage.

Arrived in Rome, the centurion who had charge of the prisoners handed them to the captain of the guard; but Paul was allowed to dwell in his own hired house with a soldier to watch over him. And he sent for the chief Jews, and he taught them concerning Jesus Christ, and what Moses and the prophets had written about him. And some believed the things which were spoken, and some believed not. For two years Paul welcomed all who came to him, preaching to them the kingdom of God, and teaching those things which concern the Lord Jesus Christ, with all confidence, no man forbidding him. Paul also wrote letters to the churches, the chief towns, and also to some of the younger bishops of the Church. Letters were also written to the churches by Peter, James, Jude and John. These letters are called Epistles. In Paul's second letter to his son Timothy, after charging him, before God and the Lord Jesus Christ, to preach the Word, and to be instant in season and out of season, he goes on to say, I am now ready to be offered, and the time of my departure is at hand. I have fought a good fight, I have finished my course, I have kept the faith: Henceforth there is laid up for me a crown of righteousness, which the Lord, the righteous Judge, shall give me at that day; and not to me only, but unto all them also that love his appearing.

The concluding book of the Bible is called "The Revelation of St. John the Divine, and was written by that apostle. He was exiled by the Emperor Domitian to the lonely isle of Patmos, where condemned criminals were kept, and is believed to have survived all the other apostles.

In his banishment he saw many visions; and in one of them one, like unto the Son of Man, gave him a message to the seven churches in Asia. He was also shown what troubles awaited the Church upon earth, but how in the end the kingdom of Christ would be triumphant. John also had a vision of the judgment day, and of the New Jerusalem, where the people whom Jesus had saved out of all nations would be gathered together. In that city there would be no need of the sun or moon to lighten it, for God was there, and the Lamb. And there was no night there, neither could the wicked enter in, but only those whose names were written in the Lamb's Book of Life. And many

ST. JOHN'S VISION

other wonderful things did John see and hear; and when the vision was past, the last words spoken by our Lord to him were, Surely I come quickly; and John answered, Amen. Even so, come, Lord Jesus.

The Bible closes with this benediction: The grace of our Lord Jesus Christ be with you all. Amen.

www.ingramcontent.com/pod-product-compliance
Lightning Source LLC
Chambersburg PA
CBHW032121230426
43672CB00009B/1818